FINDING WALDO

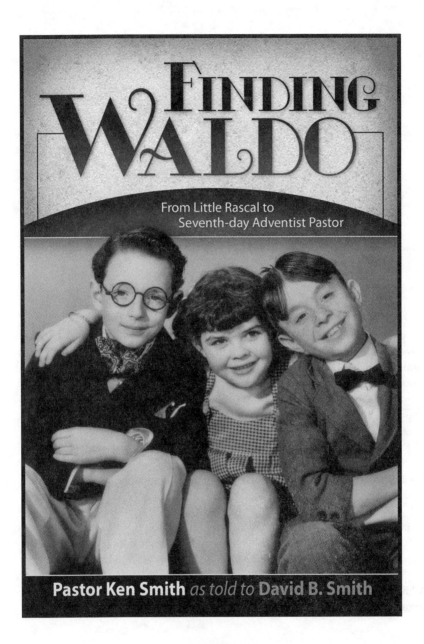

FINDING WALDO

From Little Rascal to Seventh-day Adventist Pastor

Pastor Ken Smith *as told to* **David B. Smith**

Pacific Press® Publishing Association
Nampa, Idaho
Oshawa, Ontario, Canada
www.pacificpress.com

Cover design by Gerald Lee Monks
Cover design resources from David Smith
Inside design by Aaron Troia
Inside photos from David Smith

The author is responsible for the accuracy of all facts and quotations cited in this book.

Scripture quotations marked NIV are from the HOLY BIBLE, NEW INTERNATIONAL VERSION®. Copyright © 1973, 1978, 1984 by International Bible Society. Used by permission of Zondervan Publishing House. All rights reserved.

Additional copies of this book are available online at www.adventistbookcenter.com or by calling toll-free 1-800-765-6955.

ISBN 13: 978-0-8163-2376-0
ISBN 10: 0-8163-2376-3

09 10 11 12 13 • 5 4 3 2 1

Acknowledgments

A huge "O-tay!" and thank you to the myriad of *Our Gang* fans whose recollections are found in these pages. Foremost among them is the standout compendium by film critic Leonard Maltin, with Richard W. Bann, *The Little Rascals: The Life and Times of Our Gang*. It is a meticulous chronicling of the entire film series, with insider tidbits and colorful synopses of every single episode, including hard-to-trace shorts. It would have been impossible to re-create Waldo's Hollywood career, especially several years after his passing, without this informative and definitive volume.

I'm grateful also to the unnamed fans who keep various Web sites humming with fun factoids and details about their favorite *Our Gang* participants. Alfalfa's many admirers have included choice dialogue and reviews for all of the cowlicked wonder's film shorts before the series moved to MGM in 1938. Their kind words about my dad were heartening to read as I scoured the Internet for anecdotes and a fairly complete timeline.

Dad did not go out of his way to relive or boast about his years in *Our Gang*; as a result, it has taken more than a trace of sanctified fiction and reconstructed conversations in order to fully tell this tale.

This is obviously my favorite Our Gang publicity photo. You can tell that Darla is trying unsuccessfully to mask her romantic preference for me.

But the essential details of his Hollywood career and the story of how the Lord led him into a life of mission service in Asia are all true.

Dad's story is dedicated to his family: two wonderful parents; his brother, Dennis; my three incredible brothers and their wives; my wife, Lisa; and nine young people who are proud to have had such a man as their grandfather. And at this writing, our own granddaughter Kira looks forward to the day she can meet Great-Grandpa Waldo when God has that great casting call on the other side of eternity.

Contents

Chapter One

CAMERAS ARE ROLLING

"Cut!"

That single syllable, amplified through the director's megaphone, was always the greatest sound in the world to a kid like me. The filmed scene was now "in the can," finished, done. We could take a break from all the hard work of memorizing lines, standing in the right place, entering the room on cue, making sure to look happy or confused or angry—whatever the director wanted.

I looked over at Alfalfa, who was the undisputed star of *Our Gang*. His trademark cowlick drooped to one side, even though the unruly lock of hair had been firmly greased into place early that morning by Junie, the hard-boiled makeup lady. He and his chubby sidekick, Spanky, were shooting a quick scene on a bench in our clubhouse, with some of the rest of us just filling in the corners as extras. Alfalfa had a self-satisfied look on his face, knowing that he had nailed the performance. Everyone on the set admitted that young Carl Switzer, a.k.a. Alfalfa, had natural-born talent.

"Good job, Alfie!"

Our director, Fred Newmeyer, walked into the shot, stepping carefully over some lighting cables. "You, too, Spanky. That's a keeper for sure." He glanced over to where Tommy, Joe "Corky," and I were still standing on our marks. None of us had been given any dialogue in this particular scene, so our task was basically to plop ourselves down where we were told and try to blend into the scenery.

"Waldo, guys, you all were fine. Take ten, kids."

A lot of days, "fine" was all the positive reinforcement we got on Hal Roach's movie set. The core troop consisted mostly of Alfalfa, Spanky, "Buckwheat" Thomas, Butch, and Darla. They were the elite generation in Roach's long-running franchise of amusing neighborhood kids. I got an occasional line here and there; so did a chunky little guy known as Porky. But sometimes, a whole week of shooting would go by during which the rest of us did little more than lurk in the shadows, hoping for a crumb of attention.

Alfalfa sauntered over, traces of pancake makeup beginning to streak down his cheek as he perspired under the hot klieg lights. He was wearing a brown suit that had a stain on the left sleeve, the kind of casual blotch that didn't really show up in black-and-white reels, plus his trademark bow tie. His face was covered with freckles, and he had an endearing gap between his two front teeth.

"Hey, Dagwood," he said to me without any trace of animosity. "Fetch me a doughnut, would ya?"

I flushed with resentment. The doughnut cart was clear over on the adjacent soundstage; it was a good five-minute hike there and back. More irritating was the fact that Alfalfa enjoyed flustering me by purposely butchering my name.

My parents, George and Donna Smith, had confounded all of their friends in Colorado by naming their firstborn son Darwood. Where they got the unique name, I have no idea. Even as a toddler, I remember hating it. In the movie biz, though, it actually worked nicely. My publicity head shot listed me as "Darwood Kaye, child star," and showed a thoughtful-looking kid with a gorgeous head of curly dark hair and a wistful half smile. It wasn't official, of course, but I wasn't going to get anywhere in Tinseltown with a last name like Smith. So "Darwood Kaye" was fine. (Thinking about it years later, I wondered whether studio agents thought I was a precocious nephew of movie star Danny Kaye—except that he didn't really break through until the early 1940s, and those of us in *Our Gang* were already working hard here in 1937.) I was getting regular work in various movie projects as word got around that Darwood Kaye was a compliant and decently talented child actor.

But Alfalfa took perverse delight in calling me Dagwood, after the inept sleep-deprived husband in the *Blondie* cartoon strip Chic Young had begun drawing seven years earlier. Now in 1937, "Dagwood" was the butt of a lot of jokes, and Alfalfa never tired of the gag. "Hey, Dagwood, what did you and Blondie do last weekend?" "Hey, Dag, did the old lady make you practice the piano all day Sunday?"

I sighed and began the hike to the doughnut cart. Part of me wished I had the guts to punch Alfalfa right in his freckled nose; the smarter part of me realized that getting along with Hal Roach's pet might earn me some meatier roles in upcoming shows they called "two-reelers." I grabbed two fresh doughnuts from Mags, a woman so hugely obese that the grip and lighting assistants openly joked that she must be Spanky's aunt. Mags oversaw the pastries and other refreshments that the cast and crew enjoyed during their long, and usually tedious, workdays.

"How ya doin', hon?" She gave me a cheerful wink. "That Alfalfa behaving himself?"

"He's being OK."

She emitted a short, sarcastic laugh, raspy from cigarette smoke. "That'd be the first time." She glanced down at her blouse, stained with a dribble of strawberry filling from one of the jelly doughnuts. "What a scamp! I don't know how the rest of you kids put up with him." She reached for a cup. "Want a Coke, too, sugar?" *Our Gang* kids consumed free Coca-Cola like it was water.

I accepted the soda and juggled the snacks on my way back to the *Our Gang* set. Alfalfa and Spanky were both sitting on the rungs of a ladder leading to a loft where extra sets were stored. Shrugging, Alfalfa accepted the sugary pastry without a "Thank you," as if the honor of waiting on him should be reward enough. He took one big chomp on the confection and then jumped to his feet.

"Hey, fat guy, watch this." Spanky, who was as round as he was tall, didn't seem to mind the insult at all. He was a seasoned pro in the moving pictures, having occupied a central role on *Our Gang* for six years already. Talent scouts had found the roly-poly wonder at the tender age of three, and Spanky had an endearing beatific smile that lit up the screen and belied his impish pranks. Kids all around North America were spending their nickels every Saturday morning to watch *Our Gang* two-reel episodes, in which Spanky dreamed up comical adventures and tormented the adults in the stories. Grown-ups were even picking up and using his trademark expression, "Okey-dokey," at the office and corner drugstore.

Alfalfa carefully set his partially eaten doughnut on the bottom rung of the ladder and held both hands up, waist high. "A one, a two, a one-two-three," he muttered in his cracking soprano voice. With a dip, he did a tap dance move, his scruffy shoes making sharp little *pops* on the concrete floor of the stage. "Ack! I busted it!" he spat out, as his feet got tangled on the last part of the routine. "Here; watch." Taking another quick bite of the doughnut, he flawlessly ran through the thirty-second dance move.

"I can do that too." I was surprised to hear my own voice but knew this was my chance to get noticed. In the shadows, I could see some of the stagehands pausing to watch.

"Let's see it, Dags." Surprisingly, Alfalfa willingly gave up the spotlight. "Break a leg."

Mom and Dad had been taking me to tap lessons every Thursday evening for the last eight months, so I took a deep breath and jumped into the routine Mr. Goldstein had showed me just the week before. It was two to the left, two to the right, then a shuffle dip—one, two, repeat—and a drop to one knee after a flurry of clicks with both hands aloft.

"Whoo, baby!" One of the sound guys, hauling a mike stand across the stage, paused and gave me a one-man standing ovation. "Good show, Waldo."

"Yeah." Alfalfa nodded agreeably. "You and me, Dags, we oughta go on the road."

Spanky let himself down gingerly. "Dancing's for sissies." He laughed, helped himself to the last two bites of Alfalfa's doughnut, and waddled over to the restroom.

"Three minutes!" Mr. Newmeyer began circling around the huge studio, rounding up the *Our Gang* kids. "Come on, little ladies and gents. Time's a-wastin' around here. It's showtime!"

There was just one more scene to be shot, this one in our usual *Our Gang* clubhouse. We were filming a howlingly funny script entitled *Mail and Female,* and the opening scenes have Spanky and his pals sputtering because the MacGillicudy sisters have organized a lavish party and deliberately left out all of the gentlemen in the neighborhood. Bent on getting even, he's trying to reconvene the long-running He-Man Woman Haters Club. My only assignment is to sit with the other guys and look appropriately vengeful as Spanky whips up the troops with a campaign speech.

The gag in the story is that Spanky designates Alfalfa as club president despite his many chronicled romantic lapses. In fact, the cowlicked hero isn't even in the room while the nominating and seconding speeches are underway; he's out under a tree, composing a love letter to Darla. Our cameraman records the moment as Alfalfa enters the clubhouse just in time to hear he's been appointed to high office. He begins to strut around the room, appointing a newcomer named Spike Lee (no relation to the film director) as sergeant at arms—still not quite sure what the paddle-wielding disciplinarian is supposed to be enforcing. He finally leans over and stage-whispers, "By the way, Spanky, what am I president of?" When he learns that the Woman Haters Club has been reorganized, he gives the camera his classic double take and realizes that he has urgent need of a shredding machine. If the gang finds that love letter on his person, he's in serious trouble.

We ran the scene twice, and Alfalfa was his usual brilliant self. I had to struggle to keep a straight face as he mugged his way through the story.

"Cut!" The boss came over and gave his big star a comic kiss on the top of his head. "Aww, cut it out!" Alfalfa protested, pleased.

"You guys are the cat's meow," Mr. Newmeyer praised, looking up at the big studio clock above the door that led to the front lobby and the visitors' parking lot. "We get to quit fifteen minutes early." He looked at his clipboard. "Tomorrow at eight thirty, same wonderful cast of lovable characters. Alfie, Spanky, Darla, Buckwheat, Porky, Spike, Waldo . . ."

I went over to the coatroom and found my jacket. It was a brisk November afternoon, and even here in sunny Los Angeles, the early sunsets made it chilly out in the Hal Roach lot and in the surrounding hills of Hollywood. As I zipped up, I noticed little Darla Hood struggling with the buttons of her red coat.

"You did really good today," I managed, trying to keep my voice steady. Darla was a noticeable femme fatale, cute as a button and with dimples in both cheeks. *Our Gang* scripts regularly fed the idea of a childish romance between her and Alfalfa, and I sometimes wondered whether her flouncing attentions at him were more than acting.

"Thanks, Waldo." It was common to continue using a character's name off the set, a practice I endorsed wholeheartedly, considering what I thought of the name Darwood. However, Darla Hood had such a sparkling real name that she was able to use it in the *Our Gang* stories as well. She was a pixieish beauty who had literally been discovered in the right place at the right time. Her mother had taken her on a quick vacation to New York City a year earlier and was having dinner at the Edison Hotel, where a lavish floor show was underway. The band leader, always looking for an audience surprise, invited the out-of-town tot to come up and conduct the orchestra. The place erupted with whistles, and the delighted musician handed her a mike. "Sing something for us, sugar."

As luck would have it, *Our Gang*'s casting director was sitting among the New York crowd, mesmerized. He got on the phone that same evening and shouted to Mr. Roach, "Boss, we got to hire this kid, and I mean quick!"

"Do a screen test right there," the producer had commanded. "Don't let her get away!" Within three weeks, Darla and her mother had flown to Hollywood and signed a seven-year long deal with the Roach company, starting the child prodigy out at seventy-five dollars a week. The episode *Our Gang Follies of 1936* was already shooting, and they quickly wrote a part for the new girl. By the time I first met her, Darla, still just four years old, had already appeared in *The Bohemian Girl* with the comedy duo of Laurel and Hardy. Little boys all around the country were choking on their cotton candy as they watched the coquettish child actress flirt with the boys of *Our Gang*. Now each time a script arrived at our home, I scanned it eagerly to see if I might be the lucky boy to win her heart in the newest adventure.

Darla gave me an innocent wave and headed out. I reached down to tie my shoe—not wanting to let the elfin beauty out of my sight, but feeling a little bit bashful at the same time. Moments later, I headed out to the lot where parents were waiting for their talented offspring. It was a state employment law that one parent of a child actor had to be on the studio premises the entire day when a child was working, so Mom was now in the rear alley where most of the parents parked and gossiped with one another. I saw her busily chatting with Porky's parents, who were driving a brand-new tan Packard. She noticed me and waved cheerfully. I always thought Mom was the prettiest lady in the whole world, and she looked radiant in a new hat and soft pink blouse.

"Hi, doll!" She leaned down and gave me a loving kiss on the cheek, rubbing her soft hand through my dark curls. "How was it today?"

"Good." Remembering to be a "little man," I dutifully reached up and shook hands with Mr. and Mrs. Lee, Porky's parents.

"Did old Hal work you kids pretty hard today?" Mr. Lee wanted to know.

I shrugged. "Nah, not much. We only did three scenes."

"So you saw a lot of Mrs. Carter today, huh?"

"Yeah." Being in the movies meant that most of us Hollywood kids weren't able to attend school regularly. Hal Roach, who created the *Our Gang* franchise way back in 1922, was scrupulously protective of "his kids"; and a credentialed schoolteacher, Fern Carter, was paid handsomely to be on the set at all times, helping coax us through our elementary grades. That was another of the rare child labor laws of those days: we were required to put in 180 minutes of schooling even during the busiest of shoots. It was a common joke on the Roach studio lot that Alfie was an incorrigible cutup, incapable of studying for more than five minutes at a time. Fortunately, most of us were fairly apt pupils, able to zip our way through the three *R*s with a minimum of fuss. We often could knock out an entire day's worth of schoolwork between scenes or while carpenters were repairing a set.

I sank back into the upholstered front seat of our Ford as Mom cautiously pulled out onto Washington Boulevard and steered the car toward our small but comfortable home in the Hollywood hills. "So you had fun today?"

"Uh-huh." I described the clubhouse scene we had just wrapped. "They said I did fine."

"Of course, you did, honey." Mom invariably called me "doll" or "honey," an endearing practice that continued right into my adult years. Long after I departed from the Hollywood scene and had a college degree, a wife, and four grown-up sons of my own, Mom still treated me like royalty and called me her "doll."

She was a slender, strikingly beautiful woman with elegant manners and a gentle, approving voice. If she ever raised it, I never once heard her. Despite our limited income, she wore the latest fashions and carried herself like a queen without a single thread or a hair out of place. Mom usually had a car that was new or nearly new, and my dad, feverishly devoted to his alabaster beauty, worked extra hours at any job he managed to get, just to make sure his Donna lived in style. She was the typical studio mom, eager to further her son's career but wise enough to graciously move behind the scenes to open up new opportunities. She was never pushy like some of the brash parents who tried to crash the gates of Hal Roach Studios with their over-coached prodigies in tow. Despite being new to the tangled skein of Tinseltown politics, she managed to flatter agents and producers into giving her Darwood a look.

As traffic lights twinkled in the growing twilight, I thought about what an abrupt change my life had undergone even by the tender age of eight. Shortly after I came along, Dad had relocated the family from Fort Collins to Idaho and then to Montana. I have the vaguest memories of those days and the vast towering landscapes of the mountainous Northwest. But those were just brief stopovers on the

Lou, my agent, spread these fliers all around town to let Hollywood know I was ready to work.

route to Southern California, the location of our destiny.

When I was six, cowboy star Tom Mix came to Bozeman to put on a show. Dad splurged and got the three of us tickets close to the stage; and when the performance was over, he shouldered his way forward. "Mr. Mix," he said, giving me a gentle push, "my son here is your biggest fan."

The star's face crinkled into a genuine smile. "That right?" He reached out and gave my hand a squeeze.

"Yes, sir." I tingled with excitement.

But Dad wasn't finished. "Mr. Mix, my boy—he's a ball of talent. Sings, plays the piano, tap dances. He's been taking lessons and learned to read all by himself when he was four."

"Good for you, sonny." People were crowding around, but the

popular star was still looking me over.

I blushed. It was true that I had been taking tap lessons, but I didn't think I was particularly good. My opinion wasn't about to stop my ambitious father.

"Do you mind if I ask you, Mr. Mix, what do I do? Where should I take him?"

The affable western performer snorted cheerfully. "What else? There's no place but Hollywood. I run into pint-size talents every-where I perform, and I tell 'em all the same thing. Bring your boy out to Tinseltown and hope for a lucky break."

Ever since that day, it seemed that both my parents knew there was a pot of gold for the Smith family if we could just carve out our own corner of opportunity in Los Angeles. All sorts of ordinary peo-ple were suddenly finding stardom and lucky spots in Hollywood's *Variety* magazine, and based on Tom Mix's casual evaluation, Donna Smith had a silver dream for her tousle-haired son.

It amazes me now, reflecting on how so many desperate wannabe film stars today wash dishes and endlessly wait tables in Hollywood while waiting for their break, but back in 1935, good fortune almost fell into our laps. We took a road trip vacation to Southern California, parked ourselves for an extended stay at the Rector Hotel, and Mom started knocking on studio doors.

The very first film company she took me to was called RKO (Radio-Keith-Orpheum) Pictures. To my amazement, the casting di-rector took one hard look at me and then grunted, "Yeah, I think I got something you can do." A week later, I was on the movie set, taking directions from a man named Ben Holmes for a small comedy-mystery entitled *The Plot Thickens,* starring a screwball comedienne named ZaSu Pitts. She had a repeat role as an amateur detective named Hil-degarde Withers; I remember that it was set in a museum and had a policeman who kept pulling out a little book and reading everybody their horoscopes. My only job was to be a stand-in for a sixty-year-old midget who appeared in one scene.

Within weeks, Darwood Kaye was officially represented by the Mitchell Gertz Agency that had ties to all the major film lots; eight-by-ten glossies of me were spread around town, and I even had a short résumé. Dad dashed back to Bozeman, quit his job with Montgomery Ward, and returned to bluff his way into a new position as sales assistant for the Fuller Brush Company. He filled out the paperwork to get me registered with movieland's Central Casting, and smallish jobs in various theatrical projects began coming my way. My agent, happy for his 15 percent cut, cheerfully sent me out to read for anything from comedy shorts to bit walk-on roles in big, sometimes vulgar, crime dramas. If I was an extra, there wasn't much to it except to arrive on time—Mom made sure of that—and not have peanut butter on my face. If I managed to get a line or two of dialogue, my parents drilled me over our pot roast suppers until I could deliver the words without hesitation.

"Speak right up," Dad advised, directing me to have eye contact with him. "Too many kids don't know how to say their lines; they mumble into their shoes. Let that director know you're ready for business. Don't be shy."

Even as a boy of seven, I remember being absolutely mesmerized by the luminous beauty who played the lead in my second film, *Quality Street*. The picture got poor reviews—not my fault, I'm sure—but that didn't hurt the career of its main starlet, a young Hollywood lovely named Katherine Hepburn. I had just the tiniest of roles, but it was still exciting to be on the same set with someone who oozed feminine appeal and charisma.

Mom pulled the Ford into our small garage in a quiet suburb a few miles away from the hub of the motion picture industry. Dad had just gotten home ahead of us, and I could see the porch light twinkling in the November chill.

"Hiya, doll," he said, setting down the newspaper as we walked in. "Did you make a million for me today?"

We all laughed together. Even though it doesn't sound like so much now, it was quite something for a little boy of eight to be bringing home a fistful of dollars daily. The tiniest of parts on *Our Gang* paid the whopping sum of six dollars a day, which was a power of money in the lean year of 1937. Being a bit farther up the pay scale, as I was, I still remember that I was earning $8.09 each and every day I went to work in that ZaSu Pitts film. The joke later was that my parents pocketed the eight dollars, and I was allowed to keep the nine cents as an allowance. But in those hard years, we were hugely thankful for the dollars that flowed out of the popular franchise and into the Smith bank account. Every morning, Monday through Friday, the front studio parking lot was crowded with desperate, unemployed stagehands and grips who would gladly accept a twelve-hour shift for five dollars. When I signed on with Mr. Hal Roach, my starting pay immediately jumped to fifty dollars a week. I didn't find out until much later that *Our Gang's* higher-up talents, such as Darla Hood, were taking home an eye-popping seventy-five dollars every Friday afternoon.

We sat down to supper, and there was the slightest moment of odd hesitation. For years, Mom had lived in a devout Christian home in which the family said grace before every meal. Her dad, Cyrus Reuben Kite, was a stalwart Adventist minister who fervently loved the Lord and led the family in worship each day. He was a pioneer in evangelizing Colorado back at the turn of the twentieth century. As a restless teenaged girl, somehow Mom had grown tired of religion; the prayers and the Sabbath keeping rules bored and irritated her. By the time she married, religious practices such as a simple prayer before meals were almost-forgotten relics. We Smiths were a self-reliant island; all she could count on were the dollars from Hal Roach Studios,

Dad's job, and her own talents and drive. There was no heaven to back things up as far as she was concerned. But there were still these moments when she seemed to sense that nagging gap of spirituality in our family life.

Me? I didn't know anything different. I plopped a big helping of chicken salad onto my plate and began to eat like a man with herculean earning power.

Chapter Two

Screen Test

"Dad, I don't want to play a sissy!"

Let me backtrack and tell you how this dream of an offer came into my life. It was a rainy Wednesday in November of 1936; I had just celebrated my seventh birthday two months earlier and was having a lot of fun doing bit parts in films and what the movie industry back then called "shorts." Theaters drew customers into their darkened auditoriums by offering, first of all, the big-screen thrillers and zany comedies of that era. Sound pictures had been in vogue for only about a decade, and all of America seemed to want to go to the movies. But for an admission price of twenty-five or fifty cents, a serious moviegoer wanted to see more than just a single eighty-five-minute film. So Warner Brothers and Paramount and the other big players in Hollywood began to tack on short comedy stories, newsreels, cartoons, anything that would fill an entire evening and get audiences back the following weekend.

A young visionary who had already struck gold in this town of dreams come true was named Hal Roach. In his early twenties, he had made a whole boatful of cash from fishing in the Yukon and had then migrated to Hollywood, looking for new adventures. He paid his dues doing odd jobs and flattering the right people, and soon was influential enough to make his own deals. As a producer, he seemed to know how to put his finger into just the right pies; two hot, young talents were part of his troupe—their names were Stan Laurel and Oliver Hardy. The duo was making both shorts and features such as *Sons of the Desert* for their affable but perfectionist boss, and Roach was looking around for new worlds to conquer.

So, as the story around town went, he had spent a tiresome afternoon in his cavernous office down at the studio, trying to ferret out a new child star for a picture he had decided to produce. An aggressive mom came into the complex of offices with her young daughter in tow. As he told the story later, the little girl was "overpainted," wore high heels, and affected a prissy adult manner, trying to convince him she was the newest incarnation of Mary Pickford, one of silent film's most important actresses. Her stale and counterfeit performance left Roach feeling uncharacteristically weary. Why couldn't movies be more natural? Why couldn't kids just be kids? This was pathetic!

He happened to glance out the window just then and was riveted by a scene across the street at a lumberyard. Five or six neighborhood children had picked up some sticks of wood, and were jousting with them. He opened the window and heard two of them arguing about whose stick was longer. Who had grabbed that "really nice one" first? "Give it back!" "Make me!" "All right, I will." "Yeah, good luck." The banter and the brawling were natural, unaffected, and pure in a delightful and human kind of way. Roach glanced at his watch and was amazed to realize that fifteen minutes had gone by in a flicker.

"Why can't we capture *that*?" he began to ask his production assistants and friends. "Just kids being kids." Soon word went out throughout the suburbs of Hollywood that Hal Roach was going to launch a groundbreaking new film adventure called *Our Gang*—"just kids, tattered and full of spirits," as one reviewer put it later.

Over the next twenty-two years, Hal Roach and his successors at the MGM (Metro-Goldwyn-Mayer) studio churned out a whopping 221 of the hugely popular stories, by far the most prolific theatrical film series in Hollywood history. Beginning in the era of silent films, the campy black-and-white adventures launched the film careers of dozens of talented child stars and coalesced a vast army of kids and parents who enthusiastically passed their allowance and lunch money nickels over to theater ticket agents so they could see the latest mishaps of Jackie Cooper, Allen "Farina" Hoskins, and Dinah the Mule.

But the truly golden time for Roach's *Little Rascals* began around 1930, when sound invaded the theaters of America. Before that, all of the *Our Gang* stories were silent dramas, with plenty of mugging for the camera and cue cards inserted to keep the audience informed about the plot. The silent shorts were generally filmed with two cameras rolling simultaneously, often from different angles and even varying speeds. This allowed Roach to have separate negative "masters" for domestic and overseas distribution. Decades later, a popular film would sometimes surface with these varying edits, providing a distinctly unique look.

During the last three years of the silent era, *Our Gang* shorts went out to theaters with an accompanying phonographic disc that the theater operator could synchronize to match with the film. Interestingly, these first records played from the center out. There was no dialogue back then, but the music and comedic sound effects made the stories fun to watch. Mr. Roach delighted in adding snoring noises and bird chirps whenever something heavy landed on an actor's head. However, in late 1929, for the first time, a three-reel special entitled *Small Talk* brought children's voices and laughter and dogs barking right into the stories that were mesmerizing a new generation of American youngsters.

For a brief period of time, there were two competing systems of sound delivery. Some theaters continued to use the phonographs,

which was a Warner Brothers patent called Vitaphone. Theater owners liked it because it was simple and cheap to install, even though the
records were often broken in the mail. Keeping the sound synced to
the action was an ongoing challenge as well. But soon Fox's newer
concept, Movietone, won out, as technicians mastered the art of im-
printing the sound track right onto to the film stock itself.

This new A-list era for Hal Roach's pet project also featured what
some still call the best cast to ever fill the *Our Gang* roster. George
"Spanky" McFarland and Carl "Alfalfa" Switzer were the core players in
this robust troupe, with Darla Hood, William "Buckwheat" Thomas,
Tommy "Butch" Bond, Gordon "Porky" Lee, and Sidney "the Woim"
Kibrick, filling out the scenes. Plus, of course, Pete the Pup, a mangy-
looking mongrel who actually wore more makeup than any other
actor on the set—a carefully drawn black circle around one eye. (I
didn't find out until decades later that this mutt got paid $125 a
week—more than most of the rest of us, I kid you not!—and Pete got
yearly $25 raises until he was tucking away $225 a week in a strong-
box buried under his doghouse.)

In the earlier years, there had been very little scripting. With silent
pictures, there was no dialogue to worry about; half the kids couldn't
read anyway. Directors simply explained the scenes to the children,
showed them what they wanted, and yelled, "Action!" into a megaphone. For the sake of cost control, scenes were typically shot conve-
niently out of order and then assembled in an edit bay. But now, with
the arrival of talkies, this new acting team was expected to learn their
lines, master the art of punning, be sarcastic, and mangle words to
comedic effect—technically called malapropism. I still remember one
of my meatier roles, *Came the Brawn,* in which Spanky warns Alfalfa
that he's about to go into a boxing match against the Masked Marvel,
"who has never been defeated." Alfalfa sniffs disdainfully, "That
doesn't phrase me a bit!"

With witticisms like those, and with the need to now be much more involved in crafting a clever story, some of the brightest script-writers in Hollywood were helping Roach concoct these newest plots. Roach himself was a brilliant and creative man who was always coming up with funny new film possibilities. While driving to work or just while walking through his own neighborhood, he was end-lessly popping up with gag ideas. He wasn't the type, though, to sit down and grind through the hard work of fleshing out the jokes, hence his need for a diligent support staff of writers and camera wiz-ards. A young wordsmith named Frank Capra penned some of *Our Gang* stories before moving on to make blockbusters like *It's a Won-derful Life* and *Mr. Smith Goes to Washington*. (He even hosted the Academy Awards the same year I began acting in pictures.) Along with clever screenwriters, the Roach studio was confident they had the most talented children that nationwide talent searches could un-cover.

For the first couple of years in the new and exciting talkie era, Mr. Roach was actually making stories that would play in a number of foreign markets. No longer could translated cue cards tell the tale. So these pint-sized actors, once they had wrapped a scene in English, would take a deep breath, comb their hair again, and then run through the same scene a second, third, and possibly fourth and fifth time—now in Spanish, French, German, and Italian.[1] Foreign words, pho-netically spelled in large letters on blackboards out of camera range, would prompt them as they stumbled through the overseas versions. Fortunately, the art of dubbing soon relieved the *Our Gang* toddlers of this additional chore. In any case, Roach estimated that the invention of sound immediately tacked on a 20 percent surcharge to each of his films.

Now, as my agent was explaining to Dad in the living room, Roach was possibly looking for another character type: a rich, snooty kid who would wear silk suits, have manicured nails, and speak proper English. This was a favorite gambit of Roach's, the agent observed, to set these normal, dirt-covered kids against a wealthy, putting-on-airs resident antagonist, who would carry around books of poetry and quail at the sight of blood.

"I think you could do it easy, Darwood," Mr. Sherril put in, addressing me directly. I was sitting next to Mom on our couch covered with its big pale-green flowers. "Don't you?"

"I . . . uh . . . I don't know." For once I was forgetting Dad's counsel to always speak up and be positive. "Can't I just be one of the regular kids?"

"Course he can do it." Dad almost interrupted me, booming out a definitive reply, trying to quell any doubts in Mr. Sherril's mind. "He can play any part you want, this kid." He reached over and slapped my knee. "Here. Start crying. Show this man what a fake sissy you can be."

"Well," Mr. Sherril said, "I can get us a reading next Saturday. And, of course, Roach already knows Darwood."

"That's true," Mom mused. Even though I had played only a small walk-on role in the ZaSu Pitts movie a year earlier, Hal Roach had a long friendship with the actress, using her in some of his two-reel shorts along with another performer named Thelma Todd. Several times the busy executive had taken time to come onto the RKO set and meet all the stars and extras. "We're looking good," he would always chortle, clapping his hands together energetically. "Oscars for everybody!" It had been good for a laugh on the stage because the uneven script was nowhere near the quality it took to be considered for an Academy Award, but the producer's optimism had been infectious. It was easier to think about having a screen test in front of a familiar face.

Lew picked up his hat and stood to his feet. "So I'll put you down? Saturday at three?"

I reached out and shook his hand. "Sure."

"Attaboy." Mr. Sherril turned to Dad. "I got a good feeling about this one. First of all, Darwood can play the part in his sleep."

"Yeah."

Without thinking, the agent pulled out a pack of cigarettes and lit a smoke. "Plus, Roach has a little bit of a tendency to grab people he already knows. Not so much now as when the series first started, though. I guess back in twenty-two, they drafted their first kids by just taking all the nephews and cousins of people who worked in the business. It was a real family affair back then. I guess that first gal they used—pretty little thing named Mary Kornman—was just the daughter of Hal's still photographer. These days, we sometimes got three hundred kids coming over to Culver City to try out for these parts. From Florida, New York, everywhere." He reached out and gave my hair a tentative mussing. "But Roach already knows us, and I talked to one of the AD's who said he'd put in a good word for us." He picked a stray piece of lint off his suit, then caught himself. "Sorry, that's 'assistant director.' "

"Oh, we know." Mom's laugh was silvery. "We're fast learners in this house. What's the character name?" she wanted to know.

The man grinned, "Waldo." He chuckled, "Sounds like a girlie boy already, don't it?" He made a little money-money-money gesture with his thumb and fingers, as if playing with a deliciously large roll of bills. "But, hey, it all pays the same. Waldo, my simpering friend, you're gonna make your mommy and daddy very, very rich. You just show up with a starched silk collar and let old Roach see you cry on cue."

For the next week, Mom and Dad rehearsed with me during supper and after my homework was finished. I tried to develop a little pout and give my eyebrows a disdainful arch, as if to imply, "What a bunch of idiots! From under what rock did you crawl out?"

"No, not that much!" Mom scolded, trying to keep me from going over the top in my affectation. "Just a little arch. Like that," she nodded as I put the slightest sniff into my gaze. "Uh-huh. There you go, hon."

Her eyes twinkled as she told me of a cousin she remembered as a teenage girl back in Colorado. "We'd sit together in church every Sabbath, and she would just put on the worst airs you ever saw. Right while Daddy was preaching the sermon she would be catching the eye of this boy—and then right when he saw her, she'd turn away." She laughed. "I don't think Eleanor ever did give him the time of day." She cocked her head, remembering. "So just do like that."

It seemed like a thin connection to my upcoming role, but I tried to imagine people wanting my autograph and having to say in a stuffy, impatient voice: "Not right now, sorry. My chauffeur is bringing the car round front, and I really can't spare a moment." Even though the Smith family would never in a million years have a chauffeur, and even though we still scoured restaurant menus for the cheapest possible items and never ordered a soda or juice with our meals, it was fun to pretend I was special.

Saturday morning I dawdled over breakfast, trying not to be nervous. I knew talent scouts didn't like it when kids were cocksure and arrogant, but it was worse to be trembly and self-effacing. I'd heard that Hollywood chewed up people who were timid or afraid.

The mailman came, and Mom sorted through the magazines and advertisements. She was wearing a pair of pretty lavender slacks and a lacy white blouse; I felt a surge of boyish pride that she could compete with the dazzling actresses I sometimes saw on the movie sets.

"Here you go, doll," she handed me a long envelope. "From Grandpa."

I tore the letter open eagerly. Grandpa Reuben Kite lived far away, and I hadn't seen him since I was five. But at least once a month, he sent me a newsy, fun letter that was filled with stories and bits of humor. I pictured preachers being all stuffy and bossy, but Grandpa's letters weren't like that at all. This one was three pages long, filled with a neat, masculine print that was easy to read. He described in detail how a farmer's sheep had wandered into the church sanctuary one Sabbath and moseyed up to the altar right while a soloist was singing a hymn called "Come to the Foot of the Cross." "I got up after she was done," Grandpa wrote, "and said, 'Now, folks, if a farm animal knows enough to come to Jesus and be saved, why not the rest of us?' And two people actually came forward!" I grinned, picturing the scene.

Right at the end, he added a little note. "Darwood, I hope you know how often your grandma and I think of you and pray for you. I know it's exciting being in Hollywood and getting to be in movies. But I have a little secret for you. I have this feeling—maybe God is whispering in my ear—but I just think He has something amazing He's going to have you do for Him one of these days."

It was signed, as always, "Love, your old Grandpa." Then a P.S. "Hey, kiddo, I read the most wonderful storybook the other day. It was about a missionary man and his wife who went to China and built a hospital for the people there. Full of stories! When Grandma finishes reading it, I'm going to send it out for you to enjoy. OK?"

He was always doing stuff like that. When I turned six, he had mailed me a Bible with a leather binding that even had my name engraved on it. And if he saw interesting magazine articles or books, he would stick stamps all over them and mail them out to his "famous grandson." I sometimes wondered if Mom minded that Grandpa was sneaking some religion into my busy life, but she never seemed to care. If hearing from Grandpa made me happy, that was fine with her.

That afternoon Dad drove me over to the expansive Hal Roach complex in Culver City. The main offices were covered with carefully groomed ivy, and the place was already a local tourist attraction. The parking lot was half filled even on a weekend, and several bored taxi drivers loitered near the entrance, hoping for a wealthy fare to come along needing a ride to Rodeo Drive. We found the receptionist, who fetched both of us a soft drink and asked us to wait. "He'll be right down."

I had no lines to rehearse but tried to keep thinking of ways to give off airs of unapproachable grandeur. "Just remember, you're the king and they're the peasants," Dad had reminded me on the drive over.

"OK."

"Mr. Smith? Darwood?"

We looked up. Hal Roach was a friendly man whose demeanor put people at ease immediately. "We meet again! I hear you might be our Waldo."

"Yes, sir." I tried to make sure my voice came out clear and confident, even though I was still just seven.

"Well, come on up. You, too, Pops."

We followed him up a flight of stairs and into his huge office. Big photos of his successful projects covered the walls. Laurel and Hardy. *Our Gang.* There was a picture of Jackie Cooper, who had gone from the Roach comedies into a hugely successful career in feature films. Against the other wall were more posters of thrillers Mom and Dad would never in a million years let me go see. The place reeked of success and power.

Hal Roach sat down and looked me over. "Well, son, you know what we're looking for, but let me describe it again. You know about the *Gang,* of course."

"Yes, sir."

"Just kids having fun. Lost dogs. Making the teacher mad. Putting a frog in Alfalfa's pants. Stuff like that. Putting on shows to raise money for this silly thing or that."

"Uh-huh."

He drummed on his desk. "But we need a smarty-pants to play these ragamuffins *against*. When they spell everything wrong and get their *s*'s backward all the time, it'd be a gas to have Mr. Shakespeare right in the thick of it, saying, 'Come on, chums, that's not quite cricket, don't you know?' " He paused. "Not with the Limey accent, you understand. But that kind of attitude. 'I'm too good for you, but, hey, I'd like to have some fun too.' And in the end, we get Waldo up on that rickety go-cart with all the other kids. Get his French cuffs torn off."

"Hmm." Dad uncrossed his legs. "So there's a kind of 'everybody's alike, we're all brothers' thing to it all."

"Exactly." Mr. Roach seemed pleased. He doodled with a pen on his desk. "Oh, and here's another fun thing. We got this cute little gal, just dynamite, fills up the screen like you wouldn't believe."

"Darla."

He smiled, impressed that I'd done my homework. "You bet. Little Darla Hood. Cuter than Shirley Temple, as far as I'm concerned. Natural, natural, natural. But we got some upcoming stories where there's just a tingle of kissy stuff between her and, say, Alfalfa. I mean, it's eight-year-old puppy love, perfectly innocent." He addressed the last to Dad. "But it's a lot of fun."

I waited, wondering what that had to do with my role.

"So our thinking is that we want to put little Darla into the middle of some love triangles, with our elegant Mr. Waldo as the other possible boyfriend."

I grinned. This was more like it. Roach laughed boisterously at my reaction. "Yeah, I thought you'd like that." He twisted in his seat, trying to undo a kink in his neck. "Anyway, what I want from you is pretty simple." He stood up. "Can you act like a big shot? Like a kid who's been riding in the back seat of a Caddy his whole life?"

"Sure." It was the one-word answer I had been rehearsing for a week. "I'd like to try, sir."

"Good boy." He went to the door and motioned two other children to come into the office. Handing all three of us scripts, he explained the setup. The other two kids wanted to throw eggs at someone's window in revenge for something or other, and I was to express disapproval. My line was simple enough: "It's not right to do that. What are you, both hooligans?"

Mr. Roach began to explain what a hooligan was, but Dad cut him off. "No problem, Mr. Roach. My son's got a good vocabulary. He can spell *hooligans* or *hemorrhage* if you want him to."

I had never heard the word *hemorrhage* before, but I wasn't about to correct Dad. No way. I fixed the line in my mind and waited for my cue. The two hired actors, both hoping for a chance at stardom, too, put a lot of energy into their lines, leading up to my moment. I drew my face away slightly—*Not too much! Pull back; give him just a hint!*—and said in a fussy voice, "It's not right to do that. No. What are you, both hooligans?" I threw a haughty look at the girl, then panned with veiled disgust over to the boy. After a moment, I added, "Well?"

Mr. Roach's face broke into a smile. "That's good! 'Well?' " A big snort. "I love it! That's Waldo all the way." He cocked his head, weighing the performance. "And your face—it's just right. Clean skin, a bit pale. Perfect."

It had been mostly cloudy all week, but it had been Mom's suggestion that I stay indoors and out of the sun as much as possible. "Rich kids live in mansions and mostly hang around in the library." She had grinned. "Waiting for the butler to announce that it's time for tea." Apparently, the pasty recluse look was working now.

He had us try one more scene, this one with a bit more heat to it. The other boy, adopting the role of Butch, the neighborhood bully, actually doubled up his fists and threatened to hit me. "I'll give you one in the kisser, pretty boy," he was supposed to hiss.

"You try it," I said evenly, giving my lip a bit of curl, "and Father will destroy you in a court of law. Just see if he doesn't."

"Now, just give each other a little shove," Roach directed. "Forget the sissy stuff. Just bash him one."

I gave the kid a medium *pop* in the shoulder, careful to make it a glancing blow. I knew that sound-effects people, what they called Foley artists, could make a glancing miss sound like a ton of bricks. The kid backed away, feigning fear, and I took a step toward him menacingly.

"Very good! Perfect." The producer sent the two visiting kids away and walked over to the couch. "Now, listen, Waldo. You understand that boxing and hitting aren't going to be part of your repertoire."

"Uh-huh." I *had* actually been confused by the conflicting assignment.

"Here's the deal." He leaned closer. "You're going to be my Waldo."

A thrill shot through me. Dad reached over, his face filled with pride, and squeezed me tight.

Mr. Roach continued, "But in a lot of these stories, you're just a kid. Alfalfa and Spanky are the main characters; just about every story we have will feature them."

"Sure." I knew that was how the system worked. The squeaky kid with freckles and his blubber-framed partner were household names across the country.

"A lot of the time, you'll just be in the shot, regular clothes, normal behavior, helping the others make mud pies or whatever."

I didn't say anything for a minute. "Will I still be . . . Waldo then?"

He nodded. "Well, again, some of the stories won't really go into the fact of Waldo being Mr. Fancy Pants." He turned to Dad. "It's just one of those, shall we say, convenient inconsistencies that we put up with 'cause it's easy and it saves us money."

"I understand," Dad nodded.

"But when we want you to *be* Waldo," Mr. Roach continued, "then we'll put on the velvet collar and the spats and give you a walking cane and all the rest. So it'll be a story line that comes and goes."

I nodded eagerly. "When do I get to start?"

He grinned. "Good boy!" He pulled open a desk and handed me a script that looked like it was about twenty pages long. "Here we go. *Glove Taps*." He grimaced. "This isn't one where you have much to do. It's a boxing caper with Alfalfa and Butch. Funny, funny story. And the whole troop's gonna be in it. Easy way for you to get your feet wet."

He glanced at his watch. "Shooting begins next Wednesday. Eight thirty in the A.M."

"I'll make sure your Waldo is here, rarin' to go." Dad was in an expansive mood. Bit parts in films were one thing—but this was *gravy*! The Smith family was going to enjoy a weekly paycheck from Hal Roach Studios, and I was going to be on the same set with Alfalfa and Spanky, two of the most talented actors in the business. Good things were about to happen.

And for me, of course, there was Darla.

Chapter Three

Soap Bubbles and Boxing Gloves

I had to sometimes remind myself that Butch was really a nice kid. As we got set to film *Glove Taps,* Mr. Douglas introduced me as the newcomer, and they also brought Tommy Bond onto the set. He was a Texas transplant, three years older than I was, and could put a fierce, bloody-eyed look on his face almost at will. Butch had started out with the *Our Gang* franchise clear back in 1932 and had done a number of films for Hal Roach, but for some reason, his first contract hadn't been renewed. He'd made good use of his time away from *Our Gang,* finding bit parts here and there in other motion pictures and also getting a lot of income from radio jobs. Now that the studio had a few boxing comedies in the pipeline, he'd been pressed back into service.

He told us kids later that his first screen test for the boss had been very simple: "Can you fight? Can you look tough? Make a mean face for me." I imagined that he had passed that test with ease. He was definitely my polar opposite there on the set; the wardrobe department had put me in a nice silk shirt and perched a pair of lensless glasses on my nose. I had 20/20 vision, but the spectacles were to get audiences ready to think of me as Hollywood's original nerd. I could

My first Our Gang role as Waldo was in Glove Taps, where I have a ring-side seat (glasses) but no lines.

already imagine Butch and the Woim grinding my glasses into the pavement and giving me a bloody nose.

The glasses were actually an assigned prop, recognizing the fact that my Waldo character was specifically based on a previous Hollywood star named Harold Lloyd. Beginning in 1914, Lloyd made something like two hundred comedy films, and soon discovered that he and Hal Roach shared a similar vision for broad physical comedy. They became partners, and it was Hal who suggested the spectacles. "You're too handsome to really do funny stuff," he warned; and Harold Lloyd, exploiting his "Glasses Character," grew in stature until he was considered almost on a par with Buster Keaton and Charlie Chaplin, the two undisputed heavyweights of that film genre.

One of the most enduring movie still photos in Hollywood history is of Harold Lloyd hanging from a clock on the wall of a skyscraper, high above a street in his 1923 silent comedy, *Safety Last!* But now, two decades later, Mr. Lloyd's glasses were enhancing my own wimpy aura as filming was about to commence.

Two days earlier, Dad and I had gone into Los Angeles to sign my studio contract. Since I was just a kid, we had to appear before a Superior Court of California judge to finalize the deal. It was a standard *Our Gang* agreement, setting me up with a princely salary of fifty dollars a week, with regular raises to come. But there were caveats. All such deals were strictly one way. I could be thrown overboard at any time with just thirty days' notice. I couldn't work for anyone except Hal Roach, unless he agreed to it. And the canny producer often did rent out his top stars; Jackie Cooper was sent across town to make the blockbuster *Skippy,* which earned more than five million dollars for Paramount. Jackie even got an Oscar nomination out of the deal! Roach soon sold Jackie to MGM for a cool hundred grand.

Spanky also made outside pictures under stipulations that brought truckloads of cash back to the star's "owner." In fact, in 1933, Roach loaned Spanky out for a feature film entitled *Miss Fane's Baby Is Stolen,* which was such a time-consuming shoot that *Our Gang* only managed six of its own films that season instead of the usual slate of twelve.

Most telling of all—though we didn't think of it at the time—Hal Roach Studios would perpetually own, *absolutely,* all rights to the images, stories, profits, everything relating to *Our Gang.* In the decades to follow, as *Our Gang* morphed into *The Little Rascals* and created a gusher of television revenue, plus merchandising dollars, the kid stars who made it all happen never collected a thin dime beyond their salaries.

I'm still asking God to help me forgive that one.

There was a buzz of excitement on the set that Wednesday because we could tell *Glove Taps* was a real winner of a story. Tommy, beginning a new role as Butch, was going to walk by our school and

Spanky is ready to referee the great match between Butch and a terrified Alfalfa. I'm peeking into the ring just to Butch's left.

loudly establish himself as the neighborhood bully. He and his nefarious sidekick, the Woim, are ready to beat up every single kid in our school in order to prove it. However, in the interest of efficiency (I don't recall that Butch expressed it just that way), he's just going to demolish the *Gang*'s most fearsome kid. Of course, Spanky immediately volunteers his pal Alfalfa.

Alfie's cowlick almost wilts in terror, even when Spanky encourages him with the news that he has a book back home with the optimistic title *How to Be a Fighter in 10 Easy Lessons*. He begins to put his sixty-pound charge through the paces with grueling roadwork and push-ups. One jokester remarked later that Spanky set Alfalfa up for some shadowboxing, "and the first round went to the shadow." Actually, the script called for Alfie to get a confidence booster by having a preliminary round with little Buckwheat, who proceeded to knock him cuckoo in about fifteen seconds. The title of the film, of course, implies that Alfalfa is destined to go into the ring and receive some licks that are a lot more than simply glove taps.

Meanwhile, I had two simple assignments. First, sit in the crowd of kids ringside and cheer on our neighborhood hero, the Oklahoma Wildcat. The eleven-minute story featured a surefire winning theme: Alfalfa as an underdog going up against a villain it was fun to boo. In addition, the script called for the pint-sized duo of Porky and Buckwheat—their unison response to everything was "O-tay!"—to win the day with a clever *Our Gang* contraption: they rigged a huge "loaded" glove on the edge of a massive club to come hurtling through the air and knock Butch cold, leaving Alfalfa the winner. The film closes with Alfalfa giving the world a hearty, chest-beating Tarzan yell, despite the nature of the knockout. And just as the closing credits were about to roll, I got my second break: the script called for me to pick up a big bucket of water and dump it over the Woim's head. Pretty hard to mess that up! (Is this where the Super Bowl tub-of-iced-Gatorade stunt got its birth?)

Again, all of us in the Hal Roach family benefited by being in close proximity with two megastars from that era: Stan Laurel and Oliver Hardy. They were always popping by to say Hi, and their mastery of the art of comedy rubbed off on all the kids milling around the *Our Gang* soundstage. In addition, *Glove Taps* was lucky to be able to steal a couple of free songs from their current feature, *Way Out West*, which got nominated that year for an Oscar. That was a common Roach advantage—letting talent and music drift happily between projects.

Even at the age of seven, I was astute enough to realize that Butch was going to bust into the inner circle ahead of me. He knew the entertainment industry well, had done voice-overs for cartoons during his two-and-a-half-year hiatus away from Roach, and went on after his *Our Gang* years to play the role of Jimmy Olsen in the then soon-to-come Superman films. (Ironically, superstar Jackie Cooper had a similar brush with the Man of Steel; as an adult, he went on to play the editor of the *Daily Planet* for Christopher Reeve's big-screen *Superman* four-film franchise in the 1970s and 1980s.)

Again, the facade of the tough guy was one Butch could don or discard as easily as tying a pair of shoes. On-screen, he and Alfalfa were perennial rivals, shooting each other looks of pure hate. But as soon as the klieg lights were switched off, the two of them would wander off, gossiping and teasing each other in perfect harmony. Many years later, in his autobiography *Darn Right It's Butch*—a title taken from our 1937 hit, *Fishy Tales*—Bond revealed that he and Alfalfa would often spend weekends hunting for raccoons together in nearby Topanga Canyon, where Bond lived with his mom and grandmother.

Shooting for *Glove Taps* took a couple of weeks, and since I was just part of the crowd, I spent the majority of my studio days sitting at a desk and doing my school lessons for Mrs. Carter. This amazing woman, who looked like your typical schoolmarm, actually stayed with *Our Gang* for the entire twenty-two-year run of the series. When the studio sold the franchise to MGM in 1938 and we had to move to our new digs, she came right along with us, and we didn't miss a single lesson.

Fern Carter knew just how to deal with her unique brood of celebrity kids, and she didn't put up with any prima donna nonsense, either from us or from the adults on the set. Sometimes, shooting would run into snags and threaten her mandated three hours of daily academic instruction. She would put those production assistants right in their place. "Sorry, boys," she would say with an even voice. "I don't care if your fog machine is broken and you lost reel number three. You have the kids here by two, or we aren't going to be able to meet state regs."

"Yes, ma'am."

She made it clear that she loved us, and the boys and girls in Roach's *Our Gang* loved her right back. Every Christmas, I always got a personalized holiday card from my teacher, which continued even after I had retired from the series. Someone revealed years later that she purchased a huge quilt once, and went around to every single child actor for a signature. I don't think my autograph added much to the heirloom's value, but with all of the stars' names there, she could easily have sold it for a small fortune.

I read later that in 1954, after the *Our Gang* years, Mrs. Carter picked up her ruler, compass, and lunch box, marched right over to the set of a new television show called *Father Knows Best,* and kept right on teaching the three "Anderson" kids for six more seasons!

Even though my part in *Glove Taps* was admittedly tiny, Mom and Dad both fussed over me and told me how ecstatic and proud they were. Of course, they had fifty reasons to be proud every Friday afternoon; but the way they carried on, you would have thought I was up for a Best Supporting Actor nomination. On days when the filming went well, *Our Gang* kids got to stay a little late and watch the "rushes," meaning the raw footage. That particular day, Dad had been taking studio duty, and he sat proudly with his arm around me. He kept hissing, "There you are! There you are!" as my few seconds on the screen jumped into view. A big smile spread across his face during my finale with the water bucket. "Honey, you sure got that boy good." He beamed. "What's his name?"

"Woim." I blinked as the lights came back on. "Instead of Worm."

Riding home that night, I couldn't help but think once again of my beloved grandpa Kite. While I was working in Hollywood, he was probably hunched over a Bible, painstakingly writing out his sermon for the following Sabbath morning at church. What would he think of the work I was doing? Even as a boy, stray thoughts like those bugged me sometimes.

In all honesty, there was nothing inherently wicked about the environment I found myself in during the golden days of *Our Gang*. Hal Roach was aware that he was working with innocent children, and he took scrupulous care to protect us from the darker influences of the world's movie capital. Production crews had strict instructions from the boss that there was to be no swearing or profane language on the set. Even when a ladder would tip over, spilling paint everywhere, or a carpenter would nail his thumb to the wall, the language was relatively clean.

Ironically, the majority of the expletives I heard came from the most innocent-looking source you can imagine—Spanky! Despite his wide-eyed baby face, the kid had a vocabulary that would have fit right in with a navy shipyard. Fern Carter had to regularly stand him in the corner for his outbursts, and I can remember stagehands turning their faces away to hide a smirk when Spanky would let loose with a cussword. In fact, a story going clear back to 1932 had the stubby little actor appearing in a two-reel story simply titled *Spanky*. The three-year-old star was supposed to be chasing bugs around the house with a little rubber hammer. A propman named Don Sandstrom had rigged a plastic bug to a long wire, and every time Spanky tried to nail the frisky insect, Don would jerk it just out of reach again. The crew was helpless with laughter, and from off camera, director Bob McGowan kept shouting, "Hit it, Spanky, hit it!" Finally exasperated, Spanky turned around and shrieked, "If Don'll just hold the #%&^$*@ thing still, I will!"

In looking back through the archives, *Our Gang* probably reflected spiritual values and themes in about the same sporadic way that the film industry still does today. Writers and producers, anxious to strike a responsive chord in their huge theatergoing audience, realized from the outset that most families read their Bibles and thought sometimes about heaven and angels.

At times, the scripts would reflect those family values. Clear back in 1933, long before I was hired, Bob McGowan directed Spanky in a two-reel story entitled *Bedtime Worries,* which was built around the familiar theme of a little boy who's afraid of sinister noises and burglars in the house. There actually *is* a thief, played by Harry Bernard, who comes in through Spanky's bedroom window and tries to make off with the family's silverware. At bedtime, though, Mom and Dad try to leave their little son to sleep alone for the first time. (By the way, the studio never bothered to maintain any continuity regarding actors' on-screen parents. By one count, Spanky had at least twenty "mothers" during his ninety-five episodes; in this short, the role was taken by vaudeville comedienne Gay Seabrook.) Spanky tells them he's "ascaird" of the bogeyman. Mom comforts him by saying, "Well, sweetheart, don't forget that your guardian angel is right here with you." As they leave, the still-frightened kid mutters into the gloom, "Better stick around, Guardie. I might need ya!"

One of the last silent films, *Little Mother,* is a cute story in which Bobby "Wheezer" Hutchins and Donnie "Beezer" Smith, two brothers, are grieving because Mom has died and gone to heaven. A beatific apparition appears, convincing the morose little guys their mother has returned from the mansions of paradise. Actually, it's Mom's twin sister, who has come to care for the orphans. Sensing their love, she decides to permit the charade and stays on in her sister's place. Wheezer Hutchins later did another spiritual soap opera involving prayer for a baby brother he mistakenly thinks the angels have taken off to heaven. When the toddler reenters the room and bops Wheezer over the head, he rolls his eyes and grimaces while he comments, "Well, he's back, all right."

Another story, *Little Sinner,* was created about two years before I was signed. Featuring Spanky in the title role as lead sinner, of course, the moral of the story was that little boys shouldn't skip Sunday School in order to go fishing. "Something terrible's going to happen to you," warns his friend Sid. While Spanky is out in the woods trying to enjoy his illicit freedom, the sky turns dark and ominous and thunder booms all around him. Is the apocalypse about to strike because he ducked out of going to services? Offscreen, a large African-American congregation is having a baptism, and shouts of "Hallelujah!" reach the terrified Spanky's ears. He scampers back to church just as the congregation is leaving. The preacher, assuming that the tot heard all of his sermon, genially asks, "Well, son, did you learn a good lesson today?" "And how!" Spanky stutters, using a newly minted *Our Gang* expression. *Saturday's Lesson,* the final film before talkies hit the Roach empire, employed a sandwich board adman passing himself off as Lucifer in order to sell Mephisto Heaters, which are reputed to be "Hotter Than Hot!" *Our Gang* kids who see the prince of darkness pacing through their neighborhoods are suddenly inspired to do their chores and obey their parents.

As you can see, our exposure to the things of God's kingdom was infrequent and not altogether bathed in grace!

We had barely wrapped on the boxing adventure, *Glove Taps,* when an office assistant came around to each of us with another script they were eager to begin producing. These vital documents were filled with the minutest details; in addition to our scripted lines and jokes, they contained all of the optical effects the director wanted— swish pans, a two shot, and so on. I began leafing through *Hearts Are Thumps* and felt a nice tingle go *zing* from my head to my toes. Right there on the second page, Waldo had some dialogue! I leafed eagerly through the rest of the twenty-page story to see if there was more.

No, the opening lines were all I got; the rest of the story focused on Alfalfa succumbing to little Darla's valentine charms. But at least I was now going to be a "player."

Hearts was set in a classroom, and for some reason *Our Gang* kids were forever blessed with stunningly beautiful schoolteachers. One of Jackie Cooper's standout roles came back in 1930's *Teacher's Pet*, where the kids, mourning the loss of Miss McGillicuddy, conspire to get rid of their incoming teacher—sight unseen. "There's something goofy with anybody who's got a name like Crabtree," mutters Norman "Chubby" Chaney. When a beautiful woman in a hot roadster picks the kids up, they confide how they're going to drive the old battle-ax out of the classroom with a host of readily available pestilences: red ants, sneezing powder, and a white rat. Lo and behold, the hot blonde is their new teacher! It makes for a cute story and gave Jackie his first opportunity to shed real tears on cue. He sobs in shame, "Gee, you're pretty, Miss Crabtree—you're prettier 'n Miss McGillicuddy." (Prettier, yes, but the lovely June Marlowe was one of the world's most wooden actresses!) Jackie described later how difficult it was for him to learn to turn on the emotional waterworks. " '[The director] made me believe he was going to shoot Petie, the *Our Gang* dog. Next he had a cop rush onto the lot and pretend he was going to arrest my mother; and he pretended he was firing an assistant director I liked. I began to cry then, and he got the scene he wanted!' "[1]

Back to *Hearts Are Thumps*. Our photographer was an affable man named Art Lloyd, and I can still remember the intimidating rumble as he wheeled the huge camera into range for our close-up on the front lawn of our "school." I was actually wearing a full suit—on a school day!—and had those delicate glass frames perched on my nose. They had paired me up with Shirley Coates, whose character name was Henrietta. She was no Darla Hood, but the writers had assigned us together for a valentine exchange.

"OK, Waldo," Mr. Douglas hollered as we got set for the shot. "Remember, you're . . . diffident." As soon as he said the word, he sighed, knowing it wouldn't mean much to a seven-year-old. "Kid, that means you don't give a rip. You're trading valentines 'cause that's what kids do. But you'd rather be at the ballet than sitting by this goofy girl. Got it?"

I nodded. Mom had already read through the entire story the past weekend and explained to me that I was to act like I didn't care. I was Waldo! I was special. These other kids were ordinary, and I should act like I was doing them a huge favor by going to the same school they were.

I had a prop in my hand—a banana—and as soon as Mr. Douglas said, "Action!" I took a bite of it. "Here, Henrietta," I said, handing her a plain white card. I studiously looked just to her left, avoiding eye contact, in order to make it plain I was simply going through the motions.

The little actress seized it eagerly. "Oh, thank you!" she gushed. Reaching into her huge lunch box, she pulled out an ornate envelope with lacy edges and swirling, feminine handwriting on it. Still in character, she trembled as she thrust it into my hands. "Oh, Waldo, will you be *my* valentine?" She "gushed like Olive Oyl," one reviewer noted later.

I knew this was *the* defining moment for my character. I couldn't be mean or rude, but I had to let my pedigree show right here. Fortunately, the scene timed itself perfectly. Just as she handed me the card, I had taken yet another dainty bite of the banana. I swallowed gingerly and casually dropped her card onto my lap. "Why, certainly," I responded, cool as can be, as though her card was the hundredth in a long line of gifts from commoners eager to pay me their respects.

"Cut!" Mr. Douglas pumped his fist in approval. "Good job, you guys! That was A-OK. We got it in one!"

The scene was part of the ongoing franchise contradiction between the goal of realism, letting kids be kids, and these crazily over-the-top moments during which young children hammed it up for the cameras, saying and doing things that no typical youngster would ever think of. This was obviously one of the latter moments.

The opening scene was rounded out moments later by a similar valentine trade by two little Asian kids, a boy and a girl. Years later, I looked up the script notes and saw that they were portrayed by bit actors Yoshi Nistu and Yoko Kawachichi, two character players I never saw again. That was common in movies—eager performers shuttled in and out of the stories, always hoping for their big breakthrough.

The story quickly moved to its main "through line" or key plot gimmick, which had Spanky, Alfalfa, and Buckwheat swearing off girls and valentines. (This story comes about six months prior to *Mail and Female,* which was described earlier.) In what was to be a recurring *Our Gang* story, Spanky announces the formation of the He-Man Woman Haters Club and swears in his two underlings as "Second President" and "Third President." "We promise not to fall for this valentine business, because *girls are the bunk!*" Buckwheat, especially, is emphatic in his denouncement of all things female, his huge mop of hair trembling with every syllable, and his face solemn and resolute.

Literally two seconds later, Darla Hood comes traipsing past, dripping with five-year-old female star power. Alfalfa's jaw tightens, but when she turns and gives him a slow wink, all is lost. Once again, his membership in the HMWHC begins to wilt before our eyes as he goes to sit next to Darla.

Spanky, indignant over the betrayal, mutters to Buckwheat about "fixing" that Alfalfa for good. Surreptitiously reaching through the bushes to where their picnic lunch is sitting, he waits until the pair is distracted by the valentine exchange and then doctors Darla's sandwich. Soap instead of cheese, and for the cream puff, a long squirt of liquid soap to take the place of the whipped cream.

The gag works perfectly, as moments later, Darla innocently asks her new beau if he'd like to share her lunch. He takes a bite of the gooey sandwich and almost loses his freckles. "It's a bit strong," he manages, not wanting to offend his new sweetheart. She stiffens up. "Alfalfa, if you don't like my sandwich, I know plenty of boys who would." "Oh, no," he protests. "I'll eat it." The rest of the scene is howlingly funny to watch, as he grimaces his way through the entire sudsy meal.

The payoff comes back in the classroom—and I finally get to re-join the action, this time just as one of the kids sitting at his desk. Miss Jones, played by the beautiful Rosina Lawrence, tells all of us that we're going to celebrate Valentine's Day with a special song. "Darla, will you play the piano for us?" She agrees, but only if Alfalfa will sing as well.

This takes us to one of the enduring staples of humor in *Our Gang*—the "crooning" of Alfalfa. His voice is truly terrible. "Amusingly determined," said one critic, but Alfalfa doesn't realize that. Time after time, Hal Roach films played off of the comedic off-key tunes he would mangle before a wincing collection of film technicians.

Actually, that piercing squeak is the reason Alfalfa landed his plum job in *Our Gang* in the first place. Ever since the early days, cast and crew had enjoyed leisurely lunch breaks at their own Our Gang Café, which operated next door on Washington Boulevard in Culver City. It was a kind of studio commissary, but it was also open to the public. The place did a brisk business as locals popped in, hoping to catch a glimpse of their favorite star. (When I started working for Roach, a full meal of soup and salad, meatloaf, vegetables, potatoes, dessert, and coffee cost just thirty-five cents.)

It was a January day in 1935 when Carl Switzer, just seven years old, and his older brother Harold walked into the diner, hoping some lucky lightning would strike. They were a couple of hayseed farm boys from Illinois who had entertained their country neighbors almost as soon as they graduated from diapers. They were visiting grandparents in Los Angeles and decided this was their chance. Without blushing, the Arizona Nightingales took center stage in the café and began harmonizing on their signature song, "She'll Be Comin' Round the Mountain." Somehow the novelty act captivated the hearts of everyone present, and Hal Roach quickly signed both boys to take roles in the current *Our Gang* comedy, which was entitled, appropriately enough, *Beginner's Luck.*

Harold never moved beyond extra status, but Carl, immediately dubbed Alfalfa, grew to be one of *Our Gang*'s two biggest undisputed stars of all time.

Now in the classroom, his stomach heaving with a swirling soap sickness, Alfalfa launches into a painfully wobbly version of "Let Me Call You Sweetheart." The melody line lurches between his usual squeak and a window-shattering falsetto, but the sight gag is that huge soap bubbles begin to pop out of his mouth during each high note. What makes his acting so impressive during the scene is that there were no real bubbles! Even in 1937, film directors had their own primitive version of computer-generated imagery, and editor Bert Jordan superimposed the soapy clouds into the black-and-white drama after the fact. Which means that all of Alfalfa's double takes, his cross-eyed reactions to the bubbles were born purely of imagination. Actually, all of us kids in the scene had fake bubbles drifting past us, sometimes popping as they bounced off our cheeks, so even those of us in the crowd earned our Golden Globes that afternoon.

A few months later, Alfalfa's singing woes continued in *Framing Youth*, a one-reel short I didn't happen to participate in. Revisiting a perennial *Our Gang* theme, the local radio contest with a huge cash prize, Alfalfa performs a recent Bing Crosby tune, "Just an Echo in the Valley." Disrupting the melody is his latest curse: a frog in his throat. Actually, this frog is real! With each *yoo-hoo* of the chorus, the frog inside his muffler croaks right on cue. It makes for a painful duet, but one the critics and theater audiences loved.

Chapter Four

CUE CARDS AND CRASHES

Two hundred twenty-one films over twenty-two years. Multiple tens of millions of dollars in ticket sales and merchandising deals. An enduring legacy on television screens and now with video and DVD sales. Looking back, I realize now that even little Waldo was part of an amazing media tsunami. Why exactly did *Our Gang* grow to be such a vital entertainment force in America?

The central key, certainly, was comedy. All of the films were funny. Even the duds—and reviewers agree that a good number of the episodes truly stank—had their moments of whimsy and out-and-out chuckles. The creative Hal Roach admitted later that he had a very simple yardstick: "Listen, if it makes *me* laugh, I figure it's good humor."

He once related how the impulse to entertain and tell stories seemed to be woven into his own DNA. " 'When I was a little kid, every night after supper we'd all gather around in the sitting room, and my grandfather, who had become totally blind, would tell us these wonderful stories. He allowed me and my brother to invite kids in from around the neighborhood. And all of us, I mean we couldn't wait for him to begin. He would tell us the most dramatic things you could ever imagine kids hearing, and he kept us spellbound.' "[1]

When the first episode, generically titled *Our Gang,* first hit theaters on November 5, 1922, Bob McGowan simply had to lead kids through one silent film gag after another. Pratfalls, bumps on the head, wagons turning over, old people snoring, pompous people landing on their rear ends in mud puddles—these were the never-failing staples of the motion picture business. For some reason, a spilled bottle of ammonia that put everyone into a slow-motion stupor was such a rib tickler, that Roach went to the well with the same joke time and time again. He once adapted the gag slightly so that a bottle of booze accidentally dumped into a fish tank made the drunken fish lurch and bump into each other.

Roach knew that audiences loved watching Charlie Chaplin with his unique gait and the patented facial quirks that spoke more than a hundred pages of scripted dialogue could. So he simply spun off adventures in which kids such as freckle-faced Mickey Daniels and Ernie "Sunshine Sammy" Morrison got their own black eyes and spilled out of their homemade fire trucks. Some of the stories, like 1923's *No Noise,* were little more than a zing-zing-zing rapid collection of funny sight gags, one after another, very loosely tying a story together.

Of course, cue cards gave Hal Roach an extra way to tell his zany jokes. For a spirited 1924 comedy called *Cradle Robbers,* the inserted title slide confessed about the *Gang* members: "All of them were beautiful babies once—but they've outgrown it." In a swashbuckling pirate adventure, the cue card announces, "In 1698, Captain Kidd buried his treasure. Since then, 14,987,652,376,456,983 little boys have started out to find it." (That's 14-plus quadrillion, in case, you're checking; Hal Roach was prone to just a bit of exaggeration on occasion.) *A Pleasant Journey* (1923) was anything but pleasant for the persecuted young man who has to help his welfare-assistant girlfriend accompany the gang on a tortuous train ride; he complains via an insert card: "I hate children—they're so sticky!" And a delinquent child named Mary Ann Jackson, *The Holy Terror* (1929), was described this way: "The story of a little girl who was bad on Monday, naughty on Tuesday, and terrible on Wednesday—Thursday they called out the Marines."

Again, Roach comedies were always deftly in tune with current news of the era and occasionally gave the nation's religious sensibilities a gentle tease. In 1926 Roach and director McGowan teamed up to film a clever two-reel episode they called *Monkey Business*. Filled with sight gags and lively cop chases, the story focuses on *Our Gang*'s first African-American star, Allen "Farina" Hoskins. He runs away from home at the same time that a derelict monkey decides to run away from *his* persecuting vaudeville owners.

It's a cute and well-told story, but its success also derives from the fact that just one year earlier, America had been fixated on the infamous creation-evolution debate and the Scopes Monkey Trial, during which Darwin's theories were being tried in a contentious court of law. Not only was *Monkey Business*'s vaudeville team entitled "The Missing Link," but a sarcastic cue card launches the story with this disclaimer: "Darwin says—Man sprang from monkey. Will Rogers says—Some of them didn't spring far enough."

That same year, Roach had a brainstorm to tell a cowboys-and-Indians tale aboard a cross-country train ride. The opening slide for *War Feathers* announces, tongue in cheek, "There are 104 ways to discourage a small boy—but none of them work." Two years later, a movie released on New Year's Day reveals the shocking truth that small boys sometimes are tempted by the sin of *Playin' Hookey*. The silent story has plenty of imagined noise, with faked gunplay, cops, a mad chase, a movie-within-a-movie subplot, criminal villains, and even a concluding pie fight. No wonder these stories are funny! But the title card says it all: "There are only two times in his life when a small boy will play hookey from school—morning and afternoon." A spooky 1927 tale, the sixty-seventh in the Roach series, was called *Heebee Jeebees,* and the plot card informed the audience: "Little boys never have to hunt for trouble—it just naturally follows them around."

In the many years since the franchise finally wrapped that two-hundred twenty-first episode, a myriad of reviewers and analysts have delved into the enduring success of these stories. Their unanimous conclusion is that Roach's stories had much more to offer than simply gags and laughs. It was the eternal themes, the classic struggles between poor and rich, which made the stories so lovable. Audiences, often struggling in their personal lives, were cheered to see that if these kids could laugh at their problems, they could too. And the comedic pratfalls were invariably mixed in with a dose of sentimental kindness.

Except for rich kids like me, Waldo, and for the snooty millionaires who sometimes entered *Our Gang*'s scruffy world, the franchise repeatedly told the story of poor children who were making their own fun and triumphing against all the odds. These indomitable kids used their wits and their talents to defeat all comers—usually with the help of a neighborhood grandma. (*Our Gang* kids always got along great with old people; in the economically pinched 1920s and 1930s, senior citizens well understood the idea of "us against the world.")

A constant story line invariable featured a millionaire home where the wealthy couple put on airs—and had to watch in horror as the *Gang* came in and tore up the place. Snooty society matrons getting their comeuppance was a rich vein of humor to be mined year by year. And of course, race cars, buses, fire trucks, and even planes fueled by "pet power" were good for repeat howls of approval. One of my personal favorite films—and undoubtedly my biggest role as Waldo—was entitled *Three Men in a Tub* and had a ramshackle boat driven by a gaggle of geese.

Probably the greatest of *Our Gang* themes was the let's-build-it-ourselves campaign. Some of the creations defied all imagination and logic, but many an adventure keyed on the idea of these street urchins stitching together, with their own hands, a contraption that would give hours of fun. Three years before I was hired, Spanky and his pals did a story entitled *Hi'-Neighbor!* which had the kids building their own fire engine from scratch—to compete with rich Wally Albright's fancy toy one from Sears & Roebuck. Before long, the neighborhood is mysteriously stripped of all spare wheels and hoses, and a local window washer is left dangling from a second-story ledge when his ladder is swiped. As one script analyst put it, "Bicycles and baby carriages are now lame."

Trying to make a million dollars the easy way was a favorite dream in *Gang* land. *Every Man For Himself* has the band of entrepreneurs offering shoe shines to everyone going by their chosen street corner. Business is especially brisk because, half a block earlier, the same kids have surreptitiously sprayed paint on everyone's shoes. When the Great Depression came along, Hal Roach's troupe discovered yet another theme: the save-the-farm adventure. Very early in 1931—I was still a toddler in Colorado then—the first *Our Gang* youngsters pooled their imaginations in a story starkly titled *Helping Grandma.* Mr. Pennypacker, a local crook, tries to hoodwink Grandma, portrayed by Margaret Mann, who was actually a poverty-stricken character actress from Scotland. He tries to sucker her into selling her struggling general store for a measly fifteen hundred dollars, while two legit businessmen from a thriving chain store operation are on their way to town to offer her a princely thirty-five hundred dollars. Even though the nearly broke *Our Gang* ragamuffins have perennially offered the old lady buttons and slugs instead of coins when they want some candy, they make up for it handsomely in this two reeler by thwarting the villain, who ends up getting popped in the jaw by a reinvigorated and now prosperous Grandma. The film was shot inside a real

Three Smart Boys (*I'm the fourth!*) has Spanky, Alfalfa, and Buckwheat scheming to get out of school by feigning measles. This shot was adapted into a popular Our Gang poster.

general store—buzzing flies and all—and typified both the timeless class struggles that made *Our Gang* a perennial winner and also the hardscrabble culture of that era.

One more reliable cash cow in the realm of slapstick comedy has got to be the misunderstanding.

I wasn't finished digesting my banana from *Hearts Are Thumps*—and Alfalfa was probably still queasy from his soap sandwich—when the *Gang* was convened for a hectic May 1937 film shoot to make a sparkling comedy Roach dubbed *Three Smart Boys*. I was hoping to be one of the three, but a quick scan of the screenplay told the crew that Alfalfa and Spanky were going to share the dubious spotlight with Buckwheat instead. The loose story revolved around a visit from the humorless superintendent of schools, Miss Witherspoon, likened by one reviewer to the unlovely Miss Hathaway from *The Beverly Hillbillies.* The three errant schoolboys overhear Witherspoon coldly telling our beautiful teacher, Miss Lawrence, that she can't get a leave of absence to attend her sister's wedding. Only a full-blown epidemic will justify closing the school down.

Hotdog! Alfalfa's never ever heard the word *epidemic* before, but Spanky sagely predicts, "That's exactly what we're going to have now."

The inside joke was that Los Angeles had just experienced, a nasty flu epidemic during the previous Christmas season. I don't recall getting sick myself, but records indicate that half the Hal Roach staff was at home leaning over their toilets, and we actually closed up shop for a few days, trying to get everyone well. So this was a story director Gordon Douglas hoped was going to be a lot funnier on film than it had been in real life.

Always the ringleader of unrighteousness, Spanky concocts a scheme in which he and his two pals will abruptly "break out in spots." Surely there's a doctor in town so poorly trained that he will fall for the illusion that Spanky and Alfalfa have dark spots on white skin, cleverly administered with a fly swatter, while little Buckwheat has white spots on dark skin. (Critics of the series have criticized this "white measles" gag—and many others in the twenty-two-year catalog of films—as being racially insensitive. But at the time cast, crew, and audiences alike accepted the gag as innocent and warmhearted humor. More about that later.) To bolster their medical cases, all three boys are afflicted with hugely distended abdomens, with the help of inflated balloons underneath their shirts.

Then, disaster! After such painstaking plans have been laid, the trio flubs things up by accidentally going to a veterinarian instead of a physician! Dr. Hertz, who's been doing research experiments on a monkey in his laboratory, is immediately suspicious of these multicolored measles cases and decides to teach the boys a lesson. The "teach 'em a lesson" motif was common there in Culver City! As he "treats" Buckwheat in the back, Spanky and Alfalfa listen in horror from the waiting room, and wrongly assume—using the well-worn comedy vehicle of an overheard but misunderstood conversation—that Doc is using his evil serum to turn their pal into an ape. Their paranoia soars to epic heights when a monkey gets loose, finds Buckwheat's sweater, and lurches into the waiting area.

So where is Waldo during all of this conniving and monkey business? Knowing I wouldn't fit in well with their ragged scheme, Spanky asks me to stay behind and nursemaid little Porky, who's barely three. (What's he doing attending school already?) Naturally, the resident Good Boy isn't going to cut class or scheme to upend the Hippocratic oath anyway. However, the whole time Spanky and company are trying to stitch together this faux epidemic, it turns out Superintendent Witherspoon has relented and said the school could close after all to let Miss Lawrence attend the wedding. So the B story in *Three Smart Boys* has me trying to get a note to my friends of the change in plans. There's a running bit of humor which has Porky endlessly trying to give Spanky a message, while the ringleader keeps snapping, "Not now, Pork! Stop pestering me, pal."

If I do say so myself, it's a beautifully penned epistle. "Gentlemen, an epidemic is unnecessary. The school is closed. Waldo." An Internet site later observed that this is probably the only note in *Our Gang* history to contain not a single spelling error, grammar flub, or "flipped letter." But—I'm Waldo!

Not only did *Three Smart Boys* end up being one of *Our Gang*'s most popular features, but a studio poster made room for a fourth "smart boy," and that was me! The vet is about to puncture Buckwheat's swollen "tummy," while Spanky, Alfalfa, and I peer anxiously from around the corner.

By the way, all such posters are now considered collector's items, and my wife and I have one safely tucked away, one of the few treasures and bits of memorabilia that have survived through these many years. Small posters, called minis, are available here and there, but the original full-sized posters are a rarity these days.

Even though *Three Smart Boys* gave me only a bit part, it always remained one of my personal favorites and was also a teaching tool. Much later, as the Lord graciously led me into years of ministry and service to others, I had occasion to reflect on how misunderstandings and careless leaps to conclusions are not nearly as harmless as we portrayed them on the *Our Gang* movie set. How many congregations have been injured by stories heard out in the waiting room? A church member overhears just half of a stray conversation not meant for his or her ears, and soon he or she builds up an artificial controversy that impacts and even poisons the entire congregation. I have sometimes watched in frustration as schisms fueled by hurt feelings and lack of empathy slowly but inexorably formed before my eyes. People who are unwilling to have the one biblical conversation (Matthew 18 teaches us this) that would set the matter straight and restore wholeness instead indulge in twenty sidebar gossipfests with everyone else in the church.

And I learned this accompanying truth: I'll describe it later, but one of Hal Roach's favorite comedy gimmicks was the "takem," which was his shorthand for the actor's double take. You see a funny scene that startles you, and then a moment later, you go, "Huh?" That second look of surprise and then comprehension is a great tool of the screen trade. I learned well during my following decades of Adventist ministry how a kind of sanctified "takem" can do a world of good. When it comes to our Christian relationships and our sometimes fractured commitment to what we call the body of Christ, how much we need that disciplined second look and the healing it can bring!

Chapter Five

Busted

Our Gang thrived on the concept of one kid's bright idea. Sometimes, when the directors fell into the unfortunate trap of having kids overact, Spanky would dramatically snap his fingers when the mental lightbulb went on. "I've got it! Let's put on a show!" That kind of thing. But a great many tales revolved around one key figure talking everyone else into a new adventure.

In the first collection of youngsters, circa 1922, it was definitely Mickey Daniels who led the way. He had a face that was wall-to-wall freckles, and he served as the core influence who led the *Gang* from one plot to the next one.

Looking back now, I can definitely see how it wasn't just our on-screen personas that were impacted by the dominant characters in our midst. Bit by imperceptible bit, I regret to say, my own personal life was shaped and sometimes tainted by the strong-willed and unholy shenanigans of Spanky and Alfalfa.

Most of the time, when the lights shut off at 6:00 P.M., we all went to our various homes and left each other alone. I know that Butch and Alfalfa were pals and enjoyed some weekends together. But frankly, there were palpable tensions within the group that kept most *Our Gang*

Spanky was the undisputed boss on the set. I'm next to him, paying close attention as he signals for quiet.

members from spending a lot of social time with each other.

For one thing, Hollywood moms were intensely competitive and jealous for their children's success. This was especially marked in the cases of our two megastars; Spanky and Alfalfa were always jockeying for the position of leader, and their parents scanned every script with hostile intensity. The rule requiring that one parent always be present at the studio meant that there was a stiff tension there a good share of the time. Jackie Cooper recalled later that moms and dads were insanely protective and sometimes bitter with one another.

I realized that my own role was always going to be somewhat limited, and I don't recall that ever bothered me much. Being a movie star was lots of fun; I was getting my share of scripted lines and action, and I felt like I was friends with everyone there. Truth be told, I do remember that Alfalfa and I even spent a few Sundays together at his place or mine, and we generally did normal kid stuff: talking about baseball, throwing rocks at a distant telephone pole, or bugging Mom for money to go and get an ice-cream sundae at the malt shop two blocks away.

On the set, though, Alfalfa was the straw that stirred the drink, an expression that came into vogue much later. He was a temperamental kid; if he came to the studio in a bad mood, everyone there could count on having a difficult day, from Mrs. Carter to all of the stagehands.

Leonard Maltin's research on the entire *Our Gang* saga reveals some fascinating tidbits about daily life in our unique Hollywood world. "Hal Roach's staff did everything possible," he writes, "to shield youngsters . . . to isolate the kids from publicity blurbs, theatrical screenings, finances, fan mail, and the scores of *Our Gang* enthusiasts who'd crowd around the studio's magic portals every day. If an *Our Gang* star ever discovered that he was an *Our Gang* star, he might not be one much longer. Roach requested that no one around the lot show favoritism to any *Our Gang*er, and parents or guardians had to consent to 'keep hands off' during working hours, which included periods for schooling, recreation, and filming."[1]

If you were younger than six, the studio day was limited to six hours total, and three of those had to be pure play. Roach could film the smaller tots for only three hours. Once we got to be school age, eight hours was the time limit, and I've mentioned that three of those were scrupulously devoted to our classroom with Mrs. Carter. (There were actually stiff fines imposed by the state board, including possible prison time for adults who broke the regulations, so Hal Roach's people made sure to live by the letter of the law.)

Matthew "Stymie" Beard, who was in the *Gang* a few years ahead of me, later told Maltin how he remembered the influence of the parents. "Parents were there on the lot," he remembers, "but segregated from the production unit. 'The only time we'd see the parents . . . is on that rare occasion when one of us would act up, and Mr. McGowan [the director] couldn't handle it. He was usually pretty good at dealing with the situation; that's what made him such an amazing man with children. We all loved him. But kids are kids, you know how that is, and once in a while we'd get out of line and have to be chastised. Whenever that happened, he'd turn around and we'd hear him say, "Bring the mother!" ' "[2]

Two anecdotes come to mind, and both of them demonstrate how life in that unusual, insulated world worked to slowly stain my soul. Alfalfa was used to being the center of attention, and his unique acting skills—born out of pure instinct—made that an understandable reality. But when he decided to make trouble, even Pete the Pup tried to hide behind a camera dolly.

The first was a story that Darla Hood shared later; it happened during the filming of *Auto Antics*, after the franchise had moved over to MGM. As she tells the story, Alfalfa was in a frightful snit for some reason; he was almost deliberately sabotaging the filming. Usually a consummate pro, who got his lines right the first time, " 'he'd louse up every single take,' " she complained. " 'We had made *thirty-two* takes, and I guess even the one they eventually used wasn't quite right, because on the last take, with all of us hanging onto the back of the truck, I passed out from the exhaust fumes and they had to take me to the hospital.' "[3]

But the story that still circulates today was related to Maltin by Robert Blake (more about him later). Alfalfa was in one of his sour acting-up moods, and the cameraman got tired of the endless delay. "Come on, kid," he snapped, losing his cool. "Get this scene right so we can go to lunch." All of us on the set could see that Alfalfa was boiling mad at being singled out for criticism. I had no question he was plotting revenge. He finally pasted on a plastic smile and got the scene right, but all during lunch he was muttering curses under his breath. Finally, when no one was looking, he furiously chewed up about six pieces of gum and railroaded the rest of us into joining him in a group chewa-thon. Just as our lunch break was ending, he wadded the entire gooey mess into one saliva-saturated ball, opened up the expensive movie camera, and jammed the gum deep into the intricate sprockets and gears. The usually calm Hal Roach was livid over the stunt, and we lost an entire afternoon of production time as the cameraman had to try to clean out that soggy mess.[4]

Even though *Our Gang* scripts generally called for Alfalfa and Darla to be romantically entwined, he could be equally mean to her. One anecdote had him asking her to reach into his coat pocket, telling her that he had a ring for her, but he had an open switchblade knife there instead. The dainty star almost sliced off one of her fingers over his thoughtless deed.

Probably the most celebrated blowup of all happened on a fingernails-on-the-blackboard afternoon over at MGM when literally nothing was going right. The story was *The Big Premiere*. I honestly don't recall just why we were having a terrible day shooting or whose fault it was. But Alfalfa was being even more petulant than usual, mugging through his scenes and being sarcastic and disrespectful. The director, Edward Cahn, finally having his fill of the pint-sized star's insolent shenanigans, told him off in front of the entire cast and crew.

Alfalfa endured the dressing-down without comment, but I re-member that his eyes had blood in them and his face was scarlet with prepubescent rage. After the director snapped at everyone to "take ten . . . and come back in here with new attitudes," Alfalfa ducked behind a pile of discarded fake bushes and waited until the crew had wandered off. Slipping back to where the harsh studio lights were still glowing—the floor-level ones for a special rear-projection system this story required—he glanced around to make sure he was alone. I re-late this story with as much diplomacy as I can manage; the rest of us kids used the break to visit the studio restroom, while Alfalfa peed all over those klieg lights. The stench was unbelievable; crew members had to bring in two large portable fans, open the doors, and spend several hours trying to drive the unpleasant smell out of there. Not to mention replacing each of the 1000-watt bulbs.

But that was Alfalfa.

In the three years that we worked closely together, I can honestly say that I was a different kind of *Our Gang* member. My own personality was frankly not that different from the refined caution of Waldo, and I wasn't a rowdy or disruptive kid. But as the busy months went by and we were constantly immersed in this high-octane world of make-believe, I began to slowly slide into my own kind of shallow rebellion.

Around the house, I still did my lessons and put in the required amount of time practicing the piano. When Dad told me to clean up my room, I did it. But on the rare weeks when I wasn't over at the Culver City set, I began to stay out late and play with some of the rougher boys in the neighborhood.

Sometimes we'd while away a lazy Sunday night out under the street lamps, playing games like mumblety-peg with our jackknives. And I remember little card games where there were some pennies and nickels up for grabs if you got enough aces and face cards. But the thrill that soon captivated us more than anything was to wander through the nearby supermarket and emerge triumphantly with a candy bar or pack of chewing gum we hadn't paid for.

I was still only around eight. There was a taller boy we called Beany; he had traces of acne on his chin, and sometimes he betrayed a whiff of cigarette smoke. But he dared me once to go into the Sinclair Market by myself and see if I could swipe a whole bag of marshmallows without getting caught. I guess the mom-and-pop team who ran the place hadn't been to the movies lately because they didn't recognize or even notice me as I casually strolled the aisles, pausing to pretend I was reading a comic book. The aisle with party foods and snacks was shielded from the view of the front cash register, and it was an easy trick to slip the bag underneath my floppy coat and amble right out to the parking lot where Beany and his pals were waiting.

"Go, Daggy!" The ringleader clapped me on the back real hard, causing my stomach to flip-flop. "Let's go roast these babies."

There were a couple of occasions where this gang of about five of us divvied up the larceny assignments. One boy would steal hot dogs, another kid the buns, with a third boy going to a different market to "borrow" a small jar of mayo or relish. Then we'd reconvene at the nearby city park, retire to a shaded corner, and savor a wienie roast with our burned-to-a-crisp hot dogs. They say that nothing tastes so good to a small boy as stolen candy, and the tingle of criminal success made those boyhood feasts seem like an exciting illicit banquet.

Several months went by where we were extra busy on the movie set, and I didn't see Beany and his crowd. But over the Thanksgiving holiday, Hal Roach gave everyone the entire week off, and I suspected that our little crime syndicate would probably get together.

It was a Wednesday morning, and I gave Mom and Dad some excuse about playing ball with a couple of kids. There was a tattered baseball diamond just one block away, overgrown with weeds, and I figured they wouldn't bother checking. I met Beany and the other kids there just after ten, and I noticed a couple of the boys stubbing out cigarettes as I walked up.

"Hey, Dags." Beany wiped at his nose, which was usually runny and red. "You ready to hoist us some grub?"

I was still a skinny kid, but my months on the *Our Gang* set had instilled a streak of educated cockiness in me. "I guess." I glanced around. "Long as the rest of you do your share."

He snorted and pulled a list out of his ragged leather jacket. "OK, you guys." He ran down the list. "Snead, you get us the bread. Jimmy,

I got you down for tuna spread. Or peanut butter and jam if that's easier." He and his pals had organized a whole smorgasbord of illegal eats. "Let's meet at the back of the Roxy in an hour, eat, and then we'll go in to the movie."

It seemed kind of silly to go to all this trouble of stealing such ordinary food items—a more spartan diet than most of us could have had just by going to our own mothers and asking for a good lunch. But again, we were anticipating the forbidden fruit of stolen pleasures, and that was too big a thrill to pass up.

Beany had dared me to see if I could relieve the people at Sinclair Market of an entire cake, and I was sure I was up to the task. I waited in the parking lot until several families went in together, and I quietly slipped into the store with them. The bakery was against the far wall, and I carefully looked at the cookies, lemon pastries, and various other goodies. There was a medium-sized chocolate cake festooned with cherries, and I finally decided that was going to be my prize.

A quick glance showed that "Mama" was manning the lone cash register, while her husband, a graying gentleman from somewhere in eastern Europe, was in the back, trying to retrieve a large carton of kitchen items. Noticing that three young mothers with small children in tow were standing in line, I quickly slid the cake, plastic covering and all, underneath my plaid jacket. Holding it in place by pressing my right arm against the fabric, I nonchalantly eased past the queue and walked out of the store. Out of the corner of my eye, I saw the tired clerk glance momentarily in my direction, but her concentration was still on punching the mechanical price keys on the register. *I was home free.*

The guys dug eagerly into the gooey confection, singing my praises. "Man, Waldo, you're all right." A fat kid named Larry grinned, his lips covered with the sugary frosting. "This is great."

"Yeah." Beany gave me a thumbs-up. "I saw that movie where you and all those other guys stole that guy's ladder." He gave a raspy laugh. "I guess stealin' comes naturally to you and that Alfalfa."

The innocent remark struck home. I'd never thought about the possibility that our improbable and fictional tales up on the silver screen might be slowly seeping into my own code of morals. *Our Gang* stories, while generally upright, were nevertheless replete with moments of "borrowing," of getting something at the candy store and forgetting to pay, and of robbing rich Peter to comfort poor Paul. I had played my own small parts in these heists, hoodwinking our on-screen adversaries when the story line called for it.

Now, all at once, I seemed to be morally bound to a new, sinister gang, not just of rowdy boys, but of a cynical and cruel way of living my life. We were stealing when we didn't need to; we were hurting other people just for the kicks that it brought us. There was a kind of hardness on Waldo's face when I looked into the mirror. What was happening to me?

Thanksgiving Day I stayed home with Mom and Dad and enjoyed a delicious dinner, followed by several hours of reading a new adventure book Mom had brought home from the library. I had always loved to read, and even when my job at the studio crowded my week and took us on location shoots away from Culver City, I generally had a book nearby. It was a quiet and pleasant holiday, and I remember thinking to myself that maybe I would begin to ease myself away from Beany and his goons.

Friday morning, I was still in bed, lazily looking at the first gray traces of light poking their way into my bedroom window when there was a tap on the door. I started. "Yeah?" There was a scratchiness in my throat from all that turkey stuffing.

Dad entered the room, his face tight and ashen. "Get up, son." He pulled a pair of slacks from off the chair where I had tossed them the night before. "Put these on."

I flushed. "Wha . . . what's going on? It's vacation." I began to pull myself out from under the covers, shivering slightly in the chill of the early morning.

"Hurry." He gave me an inscrutable look that seemed to mask some pain, then eased himself out into the hallway.

My heart skipped a beat as I hastily dressed and ran a comb through my hair. Dad was generally the most affable and easygoing adult I'd ever met. But there was an anguished demeanor about him this morning that I hadn't seen before.

I stepped into the hallway and saw him waiting for me in the shadows. "Come on." He walked purposefully through the living room and over to the front door. There was a big stack of unwashed dishes in the sink, left over from our Thanksgiving feast. I followed Dad to the door and watched as he pulled it open.

Standing on the front porch was a tall, powerfully built police officer, with a shorter cop standing next to him. The sergeant had a billy club out and a menacing look on his face.

Dad took me by the arm, his grip tightening as his fingers squeezed into my flesh. He thrust me forward. "Here he is, sergeant." His voice was choking with despair; I had never heard him sound like this before. "I'm so sorry."

I gulped, my heart racing with fear. "I . . . I—Dad, what's going on?" Tears sprang into my eyes. For all of the bravado I had demonstrated in front of jerks like Beany, I was seized now with raw terror.

The imposing police officer slipped his billy club into its holder and dug a meaty hand into my shoulder. "Son, you're going to come with us."

"How come?" The image of that chocolate cake and the proprietor's flicker of a glance in my direction burned into my brain. *Had the cashier called the cops? Had somebody told on us?*

The officer slowly spun me around and wrenched my forearm up against the small of my back. Shooting pains shot their way up my arm and jabbed into my shoulders. "We're not going to have punks like you stealing and looting in this town," he growled, his voice not quite menacing but very much in authority. "This is a good town, and we aim to keep it that way."

He turned and paused, "Mr. Smith, I'm sorry about this." He began to edge me toward the four brick steps that led out to the street. "We'll be in touch with you, sir." With his spare hand, he touched the brim of his blue cap.

My dad sounded like a beaten man. I had never seen him look so old. "Yes, sir." His voice was barely above a whisper and trembled with an aching fatigue that broke my heart.

I half expected the two policemen to slip a pair of handcuffs on me, much as I'd seen done on some of the Laurel and Hardy comedy shorts where "arrests" were a point of high humor. But the shorter officer simply pulled open the back door of the black-and-white squad car and shoved me inside. A wave of stale tobacco smoke and old coffee hit me in the face, and I recoiled. The taller officer gunned the engine and eased the car into the nearly empty street.

It was about two miles to police headquarters, a nondescript building with spare furnishings and a bare parking lot; only one other cop car was parked there. Wordlessly, the two men climbed out and came around to where I was huddled in the back, peering through the sturdy iron grate that separated them from the passenger area. "Get out." The junior officer waved me out, but didn't touch me.

I finally found my voice. "Where—what are you going to do to me?"

The man shrugged. "Whadda ya think, kid? They say you and your pals have been thieving and five-finger discounting half the stores in your neighborhood. Free wienie roasts, cake, cigarettes." He scowled at me. "Didja think you could get away with stuff like that? Don't be stupid."

I glanced around, my emotions paralyzed by fear. "But—"

The taller man reached out again and seized my forearm. "Don't make a fuss, punk," he said evenly. "We've been told to lock you people up, and that's what we're gonna do."

My mind reeled. "I'm just a kid!" I managed. "Plus—"

I was thinking hard, but immediately realized that it would be crazy to suggest that I was somehow a "star" who shouldn't have to languish in a filthy prison cell. Even my innocent eight-year-old reasoning powers told me that. I gulped and shut up.

There was no one manning the front processing desk, and the two officers resolutely strode past the main lobby, towing me forcefully toward a large iron door. On the other side, we hastily negotiated two narrow corridors which led to a stark row of cells running down both sides of the pale green hallway. All of them were empty.

"This way, kid." We made our way clear to the end of the third corridor. The door at that end was double-bolted shut, and a small smudged window two feet above my eye level admitted just a faint streak of hazy light.

Without a word, the shorter official pulled out a huge ring of keys. I don't think I had ever seen such a massive and sinister bunch of keys; they seemed to signal my doom instead of possible freedom. He quickly selected one and pulled open the last cell on our right. "In here."

My feet seemed bolted to the floor. I began to silently sob, my shoulders heaving. "Please. I . . . I'm really sorry. I won't do it again." I could feel my nose beginning to run, and my face was damp with hysteria.

"Too late for that, boy." Without another word, he pushed me inside and shut the door behind me. It made a terrifying *clang* that sent a shiver of anguish rolling through me. Through the moisture of my despair, I could see their retreating forms as the metallic taps on their department-issue black leather shoes clicked ominously on the cement floor.

I looked around through my still-flowing tears. There was a thin cot bolted to the far wall, a tiny sink in the other corner, and a stained toilet without a seat. A foul smell from that side of the cell seemed to indicate that it wasn't flushing very well. A fresh lump of sadness threatened to block out everything. I barely made it over to the bed before collapsing.

Burying my face in the gray-and-white-striped pillow, I felt my entire body disintegrating into huge sobs. *Why did I do it? How could I have been so stupid? Why did Dad let them take me away? Does Mom know where I am?*

I slowly composed myself and took in my surroundings. It was murky there in the prison; the only overhead light was halfway up the hallway. I saw a light switch above me, and I eagerly flipped it. *Nothing.* Then I noticed that the bare fixture in the ceiling had a missing bulb; there were shards of broken glass lining the socket.

How long am I going to be held here? Is this just a temporary stop before the authorities make arrangements to send me up the river? I knew practically nothing about criminal justice, but had heard Beany once muttering something about CYA and a cousin of his who had spent nine months locked up with the California Youth Authority for robbing a liquor store with a friend who had a gun on him.

Minutes slowly ticked past. I realized with a fresh stab of self-pity that I hadn't even managed to put on my watch. It was impossible to tell how long I'd been there in the cell, but my slowly growing hunger reminded me that it had probably only been an hour or so. My eyes stung, but I promised myself I wouldn't cry again.

For the briefest moment, the door clear down at the far end swung open again, and my heart leaped. I heard male voices and a bit of laughter. But there was a sharp *clang* as my prison enfolded itself around me again. I caught myself sobbing and turned away, my mind a sad blank.

Slowly, imperceptibly, I forced myself to breathe slowly and to think. I had messed up huge. All of us in Hal Roach's cinema family had begun to think we were special, that we were not to be touched or trifled with. I thought about the casual obscenities my peers some-times used, both on the set and in my own neighborhood. Meanness and successful insolence had become things to be admired and cop-ied; and now also the growing idea that, hey, if other people got hurt while we were seeking our pleasure, that was just too bad. Movie stories always focused on chasing your personal satisfaction, and film editors were adept at quickly cutting away from the attending pain suffered by those who got in your way. Two seconds after a shot rings out and a dead body falls to the floor, the action moves to the next setting, and all is well again. This was my world.

But can I change course? Can I stay in films and yet recover what I know in my heart to be a better way? Even at the age of eight, I sensed that our little nuclear family—Dad, Mom, and Darwood—was decent and law-abiding, but without any core underpinnings to shore up our obedience. Mom and Dad knew about God but had chosen to go their own way. We sensed there was a heaven out there and that the story of Jesus Christ dying on the cross was no doubt a reality. But they had never led me to address the dangers of ignoring the urgent demands of that sacrifice.

I wondered now how Mom had dealt with her own inner conflicts between what Grandpa Kite had trained her to know and love and the convenient secularism of her life as a Hollywood mother and wife. *Oh, dear God—Grandpa Kite!* The thought of my grandpa put a sharp jolt of conscience back into me. His warm letters always spoke about my turning out to be special and godly, about the high calling that was still my undeniable destiny. I had never thought much about what that better calling might be, but at this moment in the dank bow-els of an anonymous Los Angeles prison, Grandpa's paradise and the streets of gold he preached about seemed an impossibly long way off.

It was cold in that cell, and I tugged a corner of the blanket free so I could wrap it around my legs. My mind was too jumbled and tired to make any lasting commitments, but even in this faint world of harsh retribution, I was ready to decide. *I am going to find that higher life Grandpa spoke of.* I didn't know if I could still work for Hal Roach and get to my grandfather's dream. Would it be possible to play the part of Waldo, and accept roles in which cigarettes, cocktails, and adulterous liaisons were accepted plot fixtures and still move toward the better values that I sensed were my destiny?

I didn't know. I just knew that I didn't want to be in this prison cell any longer and that my even greater wish was to find the life that would guarantee that freedom.

"Kid?"

My head jerked in surprise. I must have dozed off. I glanced up and saw the tall police sergeant standing at the door to my cell. He had doffed his hat, and his shirt was slightly unbuttoned, maybe because it was a relaxed holiday morning. Or was it still morning? Had a couple of days gone by already? My stomach ached with hunger; I had no idea how long I had been incarcerated.

"Yes, sir?" My voice was shaky.

He fumbled with a key and pulled the door open. "Come."

I staggered to my feet and involuntarily reached out and straightened the blanket. The sergeant noticed, and his demeanor softened. "Never mind that, kid. Let's get out of here."

There was a flicker of soaring hope. *What? Is there the slightest chance I might be free soon? Or does getting "out of here" mean only to get on one of those ramshackle prison buses I sometimes saw in Charlie Chaplin comedies? Please, God!*

I obediently followed the sergeant to the front area where the shorter officer was dawdling over coffee in a paper cup. Sitting on a wooden bench just next to the side door was my dad, nervously twisting his hat in his hands.

Without a word, I rushed over and fell into his embrace, my shoulders shaking with huge sobs of contrition. I could feel his own body shuddering as he vainly tried to check his emotions. "Daddy, I'm sorry. I'm really sorry."

"OK, son. It's OK." He murmured his forgiveness softly, clutching me closer, ignoring the two cops.

"Do I have to . . ." I didn't even know how to ask him. *Will they be taking me someplace else? Is this just the first of many weekend visits? Will I have to wait for the third Saturday of each month when I could have a carefully budgeted two hours with my own parents in some prison yard, ringed with concertina wire?*

"No, no." Slowly, he pulled the two of us to our feet. "We can go home."

Those were the four most beautiful words I had ever heard.

Dad paused for a moment before we exited. "Thank you, officers," he managed, looking directly at the taller one. There was a subtle and wordless message that passed between them. I didn't understand, but I was too happy and relieved to care. We went out to the parking lot, and I trembled with pure and holy gratitude. My heart was bursting with the fresh resolve I had discovered inside that prison cell. Yes, I would still go to work for the studio; I would read the scripts and play the parts. But I was never again going to fall prey to the false idea that the charades we created for the screen could be my own personal ideals. I was going to find Grandpa's dream—somehow.

Dad carefully wheeled the car out into the street and pointed it toward home. I could see his wristwatch poking out from underneath his long-sleeved shirt; to my amazement I had been in that cell for only about ninety minutes.

He spoke first. "Are you all right, honey?"

Tears sprang to my eyes again at hearing the term of endearment. "Uh-huh." I dabbed at the moisture. "Dad, what . . . how did they know?"

He took a deep breath, pausing to shift to a lower gear as we approached a traffic signal on Vine. The streets of Hollywood were nearly empty on this cloudy day after Thanksgiving. I waited, wanting to know.

At last, he explained. "Honey, it was me. I called the police."

My brain reeled, confused. *Huh?*

Dad leaned over and squeezed my forearm affectionately. "I love you just lots and lots, doll." He hesitated, trying to form his thoughts. "I heard two months ago about you and the other boys going down to that market and taking things."

I gulped. "Who told you?"

"Never mind that." He made a right turn; I could see our house on the far side of the street. "But I knew you were stealing; I knew you were all messed up. So I had my friends down at the police department take you and give you a little picture of what that life ends up like."

That put a whole new perspective on things. I was tempted to lash out and be resentful, but at the moment I loved my dad so much, that wasn't possible. Still, I had to know why.

He read my thoughts and carefully explained, "I knew that even a little while down there, and you'd know it's not what you wanted."

I chewed on my lip, ashamed and yet thankful to be with this wonderful man. "So you and Mom . . . were just home waiting for a while until I figured it out?"

Dad shook his head, and I saw a tear slowly trickle down his own cheek. "Huh-uh." He reached over and actually kissed me. "Oh, honey." He gulped hard. "Honey, the whole time you were in . . . jail, I couldn't bear it. I was out in the police parking lot the entire time." He didn't want to tell me, but he finally added, "I was just there crying the whole time, kid." He brushed away the tear and hugged me close. "Ain't we just a couple of big babies now?"

Chapter Six

CINEMA TRICKS

They sometimes say that Hollywood never has an original idea; it just keeps recycling the same stories over and over again. And our next *Our Gang* assignment proved that point well. There's nothing funnier on screen than a couple of desperate guys dressed up in women's clothes, trying to avoid impending disaster.

Filmgoers remember Jack Lemmon and Tony Curtis, of course, donning wigs and reinventing themselves as Josephine and Geraldine/Daphne in the 1959 Marilyn Monroe hit *Some Like It Hot*. Dustin Hoffman will always be remembered as Dorothy Michaels in *Tootsie*, and Robin Williams was a convincing nanny in *Mrs. Doubtfire*. But Hal Roach possibly inspired all three of those successful comedies by dressing up Alfalfa and Spanky in tutus for his one-reel winner *Rushin' Ballet*.

I had virtually nothing to do on this particular story but sit on the sidelines and enjoy the broad farce as a conflict develops between Alfalfa and his enemy Butch. Our two little half-pints, Buckwheat and Porky, each get a faceful of tomatoes from Butch and his sidekick, Woim, and they come to the *Gang*'s coleaders for redress. Alfalfa and Spanky have segued from operating the He-Man Woman Haters

Club, and now are the titular heads of the Secret Revengers Club: "Rongs Rited and the Week Pertected." (No one asked Waldo to spell-check their letterhead.) They return the villains' tomato volley with some vegetable firepower of their own, and the chase is on. Butch, revenge in his eyes, tracks the *Our Gang* duo to a dancing school where dainty girls are getting ready to put on a dance recital.

Not wanting to get killed, Alfalfa and Spanky squeeze themselves into ballet skirts and even find a pair of wigs. Alfalfa, by the way, is *not* a particularly attractive blonde. When their two adversaries burst into the huge dressing room, our heroes try to freeze into mannequin poses. "All right. Where are you guys?" Butch snarls. In one of the funniest boo-boos in *Our Gang* history, Alfalfa involuntarily blurts out, "There's nobody down here but 'cept us dummies." *Ack!* Luckily, Butch is so dumb he doesn't figure it out even then. Moments later when it's obvious Alfalfa is about to sneeze—the blond curls probably were tickling his nose—Spanky successfully distracts their enemies by heaving a ballet slipper against the opposite wall.

The ten-minute comedy has a terrific finale with all four boys up on stage, accidentally finding themselves part of the closing recital scenes. There's even a World Wrestling Federation-type moment where Butch is twirling a cross-eyed Alfalfa over his head like a fake wrestler, finally heaving him into the crowd, which applauds wildly, assuming this is all part of the show. A now-defunct Web site proudly gave this topflight story a "Five-Cowlick Rating" for our undisputed star.

I had a couple of months on hiatus as Hal Roach filmed a couple of stories that didn't need a Waldo. Then my next film, a one-reel adventure entitled *Fishy Tales*, was a clever takeoff on the fourteenth-century legend of William Tell. Once again, I had just a bit part in the comedy tale; they put me in a dark long-sleeved T-shirt and put me in the crowd, sitting right next to where Spanky was barking out directions as Alfalfa got ready to make his infamous trick shots as the reincarnated Mr. Tell.

The great legend, of course, has William Tell shooting apples off of his son's head; in our retelling, Alfalfa had the unfortunate habit of taking the apple and chomping a big bite out of it after every take. We used a whole crate of them before the film wrapped, as I recall. But the saga begins with Alfie once again making Butch mad by accidentally shooting him right in the nose. Fortunately, the huge crossbow used by the original Mr. Tell has been replaced by a safer suction-cup dart gun. Nonetheless, Butch is livid at being Alfalfa's perennial target and promises to come back and dislocate his neck. After Butch stalks off, Spanky soothes his cohort, "Don't worry, pal, I got you into this, and I'll get you out." "I'll get myself out," Alfalfa moans. "How far is Europe?"

The script notes do reveal how even in the mid-1930s, clever photographers like our Art Lloyd were able to do some great tricks with a movie camera. The bit of wizardry opening the show—all of us enjoyed watching from the sidelines as our photographer and Gordon Douglas set up the scene—had one of Alfalfa's shots flying right into the camera, making the entire screen go black. Then Douglas instantly cut to a reverse angle that had the dart speeding *away* from the lens and right onto the apple perched on Buckwheat's massive hairdo. A sharp bit of cinematography, and one that had movie audiences gasping.

Special effects wizardry was a staple of *Our Gang* shorts, and this was many decades before computer-generated imagery (CGI) began to sizzle on big-screen sagas such as *Jurassic Park*. In a really old story going back to the Bob McGowan era, Roach concocted the idea for a two-reel comedy entitled *Shootin' Injuns*. When the motley bunch of kids decides to run away from home and be perennial cowboys (and girls), they accidentally find themselves locked overnight in an inventor's "gimmick" house, which is booby-trapped with all manner of terrifying devices. Paintings come to life, staircases collapse into slippery chutes, and floors shift underfoot.

The climactic scene involved countless multiple exposures and had skeletons eerily emanating, one after the other, out of a single corpse. One by one, they glided down a banister, and then re-converged into a unified body on the landing. Not bad for the year 1925. Leonard Maltin notes that the same trick had been achieved by Buster Keaton three years earlier when he put on a nine-man minstrel show, playing all nine parts himself. In 1934's *Mama's Little Pirate,* Spanky has a lengthy on-screen conversation with his alter ego, a devilish Spanky who tempts him to disobey Mom and climb out the bedroom window for some midnight cave exploration. At the end of the story, the good Spanky has to punch the bad Spanky's lights out!

Our Gang routinely borrowed from famous historical figures in order to create fun stories for the youngsters. In 1925, Mary Kornman, the resident cute girl for the first team of actors, starred in *Mary, Queen of Tots.* There's a stunning fantasy scene during which dolls come to life, and all of the household furniture is suddenly huge. Joe Cobb has to brush his hair using a comb that's bigger than he is. And in an inventive shot, Art Lloyd captures a conversation between tiny Farina, who's squatting on the floor, with star Mickey Daniels, a tall kid who's perched on top of Mary's bureau. The initial shot is taken from up high—Mickey's point of view. Then there's an abrupt shift, not just up from the floor level where Farina is huddling but taken from *below* floor level. Hal Roach permitted the crew to construct a glass floor so that the shot could come up literally from underground, through the glass floor and up to the towering Mickey.

Toward the end of the silent era, Roach allowed a new director named Anthony Mack to try his hand. Actually, Anthony was Bob McGowan's nephew; but to avoid charges of nepotism, he disguised himself with a false name. By all accounts, he was never his uncle's equal behind the camera, but he did come up with a spectacular film trick for the 1929 story *Election Day.* There's a scene in which Farina's mom and dad are scared out of their wits and flee the town. In cartoons, of course, the zooming exit is accompanied by an animated cloud of dust. Well, Mack wanted the same effect of a real cloud following the terrified parents on their frantic exit. He accomplished the feat by renting a huge wind machine and then setting up several massive trays of loose dirt on a movable dolly. The artificial cyclone stirred up an apocalyptic plague of dust blowing directly toward the camera; Mack then had his technicians reverse the film, creating an eye-popping bit of footage where the dust sucked violently *away* and down the road out of town. *Whooo!* It was such a startling gimmick that Laurel and Hardy borrowed it almost a good decade later for their own cowboy comedy, *Way Out West.*

During the Christmas season of 1928, filmgoers spent an entire twenty minutes watching the *Gang* in something called *The Spanking Age.* A title card stated solemnly, "They are spanked if they did, and spanked if they didn't . . . so they do." But the fascinating bit of cinematography is that the entire short is filmed *at waist level,* a scant two feet above ground. Adults are chopped off right at the belt buckle; reviewers hailed it as a wondrous look at the world through a child's eyes.

I suppose the rumbling soap bubbles in Alfalfa's digestive tract that noisily burst free during *Hearts Are Thumps* are what gave writer Carl Dudley another bright idea for an Alfalfa story entitled *Men in Fright.* Set in a hospital where he and the gang are visiting an ailing Darla, the story somehow has Alfalfa gobbling down, in too great haste, a mountain of junk food. Director George Sidney then cleverly takes the viewer right into Alfalfa's stomach, where an acid-drenched hot dog instigates a fight with a competing scoop of ice cream.

One cinema trick that has survived from those early days down to the present is the process screen; actors perform in front of a film screen as a generic moving background rushes past. You can still see this in feature films and TV episodes of programs such as *Seinfeld*, where people are riding in a car. Everything is actually stationary—except for the driver randomly "steering" the wheel, of course—and the projected backdrop gives the illusion of action. Sometimes, when it's poorly done, you can see the same lampposts going by over and over; often in a western, the people riding horses aren't moving at all, and the backdrop slides by just behind the riders.

Our Gang used this effect very nicely in my biggest role, *Three Men in a Tub,* where Darla and I are in a boat together. But we had our own share of careless moments where astute viewers noticed our directors' less-than-diligent efforts. In *The Buccaneers,* one of the very first films produced by the franchise, Roach made arrangements with the United States Navy to use one of its battleships as the setting for the climactic scene. As the gang bravely exchanges sword thrusts and parries with the evil pirates, viewers can plainly see American sailors standing on deck watching the action! *Oops!*

Sometimes, the special effects were limited by the reality that, even as a hugely successful movie franchise, hey, we were still on a budget. In the classic I mentioned earlier, *Helping Grandma,* Jackie Cooper and Farina are desperate to help a nice old lady defeat the shysters who are trying to con her out of her general store. It's a race against the clock as the good guys, played by Del Henderson and Bill Gillespie, zoom toward the town at high speed in their trusty flivver. Roach decided, partly to save money, to use a favorite route of his, which actually bordered his own property out at Arnaz Ranch. A picturesque and tree-lined dirt road led into Culver City, so they shot the entire racing sequence out there. The finished film skillfully cuts between the speeding trip to the rescue and the unfolding drama at Mrs.

Mack's grocery. Unfortunately, that dirt road was so short that observant moviegoers can see the car going around the same corner five or six times.

To illustrate just how innovative producers can cut costs, Roach and McGowan came up with a great idea back in 1927. Why not take the entire *Gang* over to Europe for a wild adventure? Using the scheme of a schoolteacher who wins an all-expenses-paid trip across the pond, writers put together a twenty-minute story, *Seeing the World,* that had Joe Cobb, Farina, Jackie Cooper, and the others, schlepping all around the great tourist places and wreaking their usual havoc in stately places such as the Roman Coliseum, St. Peter's Basilica, Pompeii, the Eiffel Tower, and so on.

The obvious problem was that it would be impossibly expensive to send the whole cast over for shooting. Entire shooting budgets for *Our Gang* films back then were running under twenty thousand dollars. So most of the filming was done right in Culver City, with the youngsters pretending they were riding in the gondolas of Venice or touring Notre Dame. Then Roach actually took the youngsters' trademark clothes, shipped the wardrobe over to Europe, and paid local actors to wear the *Gang's* attire for some long shots in which you couldn't tell these were stand-ins. When the costs were added up, only McGowan and a cameraman named James Finlayson had actually traveled over to Europe to film all of the basic shots they would use as backdrops.

The bottom line, it must be observed, is that for Hal Roach gimmickry and even profits were secondary to his concern for his juvenile stars. He spared nothing to make sure we were safe. In some of the careening downhill races where *Our Gang* kids were in a makeshift race car or fire engine, there were always invisible guy wires to keep everything going in a safe, straight line. In addition, the races were always filmed at a plodding pace and then played back at almost double speed to give the illusion of a terrified bunch of kids hurtling toward disaster.

We rounded out that year returning to a well-trodden path for the franchise: the *Our Gang Follies of 1938*. Based on a huge (for us) forty-one-page script, the two-reel extravaganza featured dancing girls, Buckwheat as a tuxedo-clad band leader à la Cab Calloway, and a dream sequence in which Alfalfa wants to be an opera singer. "I'm the barber of Seville!" he yodels over and over, waiting for someone to notice his talent. Spanky, the emcee for his own swanky nightclub, announces various artists such as Buckwheat as celebrities who are now rich and "making hundreds and thousands of dollars."

As with all of our films that featured music, a mountain of extra work landed on a man named Marvin Hatley. He was Mr. Roach's music director, and if one of us had to fake playing a trumpet or accordion (Butch once had to pretend he was playing the violin) it was his job to instruct us on how to hold it; he even encouraged us to master enough notes and fingering so that the film looked somewhat authentic. He would then go off camera—the man could play virtually any instrument there was—and do the actual performing into a microphone.

A greater challenge was that when films were finished, but still without a musical sound track, the team would dump the whole thing in Marvin's lap and direct him to come up with appropriate original songs to match the various moods. He once mockingly complained in an interview: " 'The music was done last. . . . And when the writers take more time than they're supposed to, then the director takes a little too much time, and finally it gets down to the music man and he's the one that's under pressure. The time was often so short that the musician or composer would go crazy. They'd want you to write as much music as Beethoven did in five years, and they'd want it in a week's time!' "[1]

Once again, as filming commenced for *Follies,* I had to content myself with wearing my own tux and sitting over in a corner booth with a pretty little girl I don't remember, pretending to be part of this high-society crowd. But, with each successive film project, I was learning about the grueling business of moviemaking and the sometimes tedious bits of fiction we had to cope with. Club Spanky was an ornate fantasyland with lamps that looked like peppermint candy, and festooned with every dessert you can imagine. Unfortunately, real ice cream sundaes would have instantly melted under those studio lights, so the technicians had created fake ones made out of mashed potatoes topped with cotton![2] Such is the price of being a show business pro.

Chapter Seven

LOVE TRIANGLES

"Are you guys ready to meet the one, the only, the incomparable king of crooners—Alfalfa Switzer?" A huge wave of screams and whistles hit the stage of the county fair as the freckled hero bounded out from behind the curtain and accepted the microphone. Wearing his usual brown three-piece suit, Alfalfa waved to the crowd of several hundred boys and girls who had paid fifty cents to not only ride the Ferris wheel and eat cotton candy, but also meet some of the stars of the *Our Gang* movies.

"Hi, everybody!" Despite being a notorious pill, Alfalfa was always a consummate pro, who knew how to make money for his boss. "Are you having fun?"

It was a hot and humid afternoon there in Houston, and Alfalfa's cowlick had again been waxed into place by Mrs. Newsom, hired by Hal Roach to accompany *Our Gang* members and parents on this personal appearance tour in the summer of 1938. Darla had come, too, and we had a fourth along: Shirley Coates, my valentine partner, who went by the stage nickname of "Muggsy."

Alfalfa hammed it up for the crowd and then asked, "Hey, do you guys want to meet Waldo?"

The gang is about to unearth Alfalfa's makeshift boat as he challenges me to a race. The impertinence! Lovely Darla is by my side, where she belongs.

I flushed as the juvenile audience buzzed its approval again. I didn't get the same volume of cheers as Alfalfa, but I had just been in two pretty good film stories in which I was a featured player, and it was fun to be recognized. I pushed my fake glasses up just a bit and bounded onto the stage. "Hey, there, Alfalfa," I grinned, parroting from the script the Hal Roach writers had crafted for us.

"I see you didn't drown," he smirked, referring to my latest adventure in the great championship boat race of Toluca Lake.

I was ready with my rejoinder. "And I see Darla didn't stay by your side for very long."

The audience rocked with laughter at the mention of our beautiful

"May I offer you a repast?" The fickle Darla accepts a chocolate treat before I rev up the engine on my power boat.

female star. Alfalfa was always being left by the side of the road at the end of every romantic adventure, and he affably pretended to be really tired of it.

"I don't suppose it's any good asking *you* for advice," he sighed.

I put on my Waldo face. "My good chum, an uneducated hick like yourself has no chance of achieving romantic fulfillment with a woman of refinement," I informed him. "I would tell you to try poetry, but *Variety* magazine tells me you can't even read."

"Why, you—" Alfalfa scowled and doubled his fist in mock anger. "If Mr. Roach wouldn't fire me for it, I'd knock your glasses off."

The script called for me to grin. "I've got a good agent. It's written right in my contract; Alfalfa Switzer is not allowed to hit subject anywhere on his person."

My opponent pretended not to understand. "I don't want to slug some 'person'—I'm planning to slug *you*. Right in the kisser, fella. We'll see how much Shakespeare you can recite then."

That was my cue. "I did never know so full a voice issue from so empty a heart: but the saying is true, 'The empty vessel makes the greatest sound,' " I informed him as the crowd laughed again. " 'Course you know Darla's backstage right now, and she likes boys of refinement." I said the last with a haughty bit of Elizabethan dignity.

It was the end of the skit, and Alfalfa took his defeat good-naturedly. "That's just our scriptwriters who make us say that stuff. Listen, kids, do you want to meet Darla?" A beat. "You'll see that she likes me best."

"No, me."

"Me!"

"Me!"

We pretended to shadowbox, awkwardly clutching mikes and feinting at each other. After a count of three, we abruptly put our arms around each other. In boyish unison, we recited, "Ladies and gentlemen, boys and girls, cats and dogs and even Pete the Pup, right here before your very eyes, the beautiful, the stunning, the face-that-launches-a-thousand-fistfights, the femme fatale of *Our Gang, my* sweetheart." We each pointed energetically at ourselves. "Miss Darla Hood!"

The place went crazy when little Darla sashayed out in a short dress that showed off her stubby legs. Still not quite seven, she radiated a kind of sweet feminine appeal, and she could wink so dramatically that boys in the back row of the open-air amphitheater picked it up and thought she was aiming at them. I heard later that she once got a fan letter from a bashful kid who confessed, "Dear Darla, I've loved you since I was six, and now I'm nine."

"Hi, everyone!" She waved left, center, and right, looking over at us and basking in the adulation. Both Alfalfa and I clutched at our hearts and fell to our knees in mock devotion. She glanced back and forth between us, trying to choose.

"What shall I do?" she asked the crowd. "Waldo brings me champagne. Alfalfa offers me a bottle of root beer that he left outside and has lost all its fizz. On the other hand, he *is* the king of crooners."

"That's right," Alfalfa piped up. "Darla, I'll sing you a song right now if you want. Waldo, here, can't sing a note."

"No, I just can't sing an off-key note," I put in. "That's your specialty."

More laughter, and then Alfalfa launched into his trademark song, "Let Me Call You Sweetheart." The scriptwriters had dropped in a comedy line about the heat of Houston, and parents who were taking in the show with their kids, grinned at the inside reference. Of course, Darla and I had our hands over our ears in mock pain.

It was a fast-paced half hour of jokes and songs. Alfalfa and I actually did a brief tap dance routine together that was a big hit, and the four of us always closed the program by singing the *Our Gang* theme song, "Good Old Days," which had been composed by Leroy Shield, adopted for the Hal Roach franchise, and used in Jackie Cooper's triumphant short, *Teacher's Pet,* and ever after.

It was common for Hal Roach to send his youngsters out on the road like this. Actually, summer tours to distant states were unusual because of the expense involved, but we often spent Saturday afternoons performing at orphanages and various charity events throughout Southern California. Such pro bono entertainment built goodwill for the movies and guaranteed a growing audience for each new release.

It was a practical reality that all of us had to help promote the franchise in any way we could. Licensees were always coming to Mr. Roach's staff and offering to flood America with *Our Gang* lunch boxes, pencil sharpeners, and even chewing gum. Spanky was the cash cow of

With a little help from Shakespeare, I finally steal Darla away from Alfalfa!

the industry; thousands of little girls played with their Spanky dolls and cooled off during a hot summer day with a Spanky ice-cream pop. William Kellogg, the health food guru from Battle Creek, came all the way from Michigan to ink a deal with us, so that he could emblazon billboards with the slogan *"Our Gang* peps up with Pep—the peppy cereal food!"* Mom and Dad cheerfully brought home all the freebies they could. For most of my childhood, I didn't have to pay for roller skates or crayons; *Gang* samples were lying all around the studio.

The sun was just setting over the oil derricks near Houston as our company car wheeled into the parking lot of the motel. Earlier, Mrs. Newsom, hired by Hal Roach to accompany some *Gang* members and parents, had purchased pizza slices and fried chicken for the entire *Our Gang* traveling retinue, so I was ready for a shower and bed. Mom had made the trip with us, along with Alfalfa's dad, and I noticed the two adults chatting animatedly as Alfalfa and I piled out of the fourteen-seat stretch limo.

"Hey, Dags," he said, "you wanna hike over to that creek again?" There was a meandering trickle of water near the motel that was daily shrinking in the burning Texas heat. The day we arrived, the four of us kids had spent about an hour constructing a makeshift bridge out of stepping-stones.

"Nah." My shirt stuck to my back, and my stomach had a bit of a rumble to it because of all the junk food we'd downed that afternoon. "I'm pooped." I noticed that Darla and her mother had already disappeared into their second-story motel room.

I flipped on the shower and soaked in it for at least twenty minutes, savoring the feeling of having the warm water push my dark curls down into my eyes. It had been a fun afternoon, especially once the show had finished and the four of us could go on some of the carnival rides, but a sense of unease nagged me. It seemed that every time I glanced to the sidelines, Mr. Switzer was making jokes and laughing it up with Mom. He seemed to hang around a lot and flashed five-dollar bills frequently, offering to buy us snacks and souvenirs.

Mom was just walking into the room as I hung up my towel, my pajamas still sticking to my not-quite-dry body in the summer humidity. "Nice shower, honey?"

"Uh-huh." I gave my head a little flip to keep my hair out of my face. "Whatcha been doing?"

She hesitated. "Oh, just out talking to the other parents. We're really proud of you kids; that was a great show today."

I climbed into bed and turned on my side to face the far wall so she could read a fashion magazine in the dim light from the small bedside lamp.

The next day we had to do two shows, morning and afternoon, one of them at a summer camp for disadvantaged kids, and the other at an amusement park just north of the metropolis. It was the same routine at each of them: the jokes, my comedy routine with Alfalfa, the girls singing. Out of the corner of my eye, I could see my mother giggling as Alfalfa's dad offered her a bite of his triple-scoop ice-cream cone.

Mrs. Newsom was in an oddly impatient mood as we piled into the Roach limo for the weary drive back to our motel in the south part of town. We seemed to be hitting all the traffic lights in Houston; in the front row of seats, I noticed that Darla had fallen asleep, her head resting gently against her mom's shoulder.

I stiffened when Mr. Switzer, spotting a swanky nightclub on one busy corner, got Mom's attention and pointed to it, whispering something. She gave her usual silvery laugh, then clutched his coat sleeve and whispered something in return.

It was still light out when we arrived at the motel, and I didn't feel like going inside yet, so I followed Alfalfa down to the creek. We took off our shoes and hopped carefully from one stone to the next until we had negotiated two round-trips on our *Gang* bridge.

"You think kids like us could ever write our own movie stories?" he abruptly asked.

It was a startling idea. I always liked creating fanciful tales whenever Mrs. Carter assigned us to make up something for our English lessons. And Dad had always said that my school essays were easy to read. Once in a while, I had told my parents that I thought a scripted joke Mr. Douglas wanted us to do on the show was "dumb," and Dad had challenged me, "What would *you* have Spanky say?" When I tried out a couple of lines, he had always nodded his approval. "Yeah, honey, that is better. Sure enough."

I stepped off the rocks and let the cool water bathe my feet. "I don't know," I shrugged. "Yeah, maybe."

"Your boat movie was OK," he said affably. "But some of them are really stupid." He plopped himself down on his rock, rolled up his pant legs, and dangled his bare legs in the water. "I guess the stuff they have us doing in the road show here is pretty funny."

Once again, Mom wasn't in the room when I got back, and I dawdled in the shower, trying to force my anxious thoughts away. Alfalfa was a decent pal and an exceptional actor, but I didn't like having his father along on the trip.

My odd feeling of dread heightened when I got out of the shower and the room was still empty. The two double beds and plain dresser made the room seem like a spare and hostile prison, devoid of the warmth we always enjoyed at home.

I sat on the bed, not climbing under the covers, and simply watched the wall clock's minute hand slowly creep along. A half hour had elapsed before I got up the courage to peek out through the curtain. It was dark now, and a nearly full moon spilled its light into the parking lot scattered with potholes and out-of-state cars.

Nothing.

Fifteen more minutes went by, and my mind was racing with lurid details. Where had Mom gone? What was going on? Was Alfalfa in his room two doors down, struggling with a similar tightness in his throat?

It was almost ten o' clock when I screwed up my courage and put on the same pair of pants I had worn all that day. They had a tiny pink sugary stain from the cotton candy we had devoured earlier that afternoon, and I had to fumble around to find the motel room key.

Still in my bare feet, I padded down to the main level and looked around in the murky Texas night. There was an ice machine and a small, unlit swimming pool on the far side of the L-shaped building, but both were deserted. I was about to return to room 319 when I heard laughter. Easing between two cars, I followed the sound. Several vending machines were next to the motel office. And there was

Alfalfa and I hit the road in tuxes and top hats to promote the Gang franchise all around the country.

Mom, laughing and holding a cup of coffee. She set it down on the top of a newspaper rack and fell against Mr. Switzer, dabbing her eyes as she laughed. "I never did hear anything so funny," she managed, trying to catch her breath. "It was the same for me."

My eight-year-old heart seemed frozen in my chest. *What is going on?* The many distinct, naughty little moments of the past two days seemed to pile up into a new, villainous enemy: the treats, the giggles, the affectionate touches, and the knowing glances. I was a naive little kid, and yet the scene before me was overpowering in its raw and sinister adultness.

I don't know why or how, but I stepped out of the shadows. "Mom?"

She gave a start, her face reddening. "Why . . . honey." A beat. "What are you doing out, sweetheart?"

It took me a moment to realize what kind of picture I presented. I had on a pair of dark trousers badly matched with a light yellow pajama top. No shoes. My dark curls were still damp from the shower. I stared straight at Alfalfa's father; he still had a large bottle of beer in his one hand, and the other was resting lightly on Mom's shoulder.

"Are you OK?" she asked.

I had no idea how I was supposed to defuse this situation, to close and lock this adulterous playground. But I walked up and snuggled myself next to Mom, experiencing a rush of mixed feelings as I did so. Mr. Switzer awkwardly removed his hand and set the bottle of beer down.

"I can't sleep," I said.

"Oh." She glanced at her watch. "I guess it is getting pretty late. I better get you tucked in."

An artificial formality crept into her voice as she turned her head. "Well, good night," she said to Mr. Switzer.

"Sure. You guys sleep well."

We got back to our room, and I opened up the door using my key. Mom flipped on the light and eased into the small easy chair that was next to her bed. "OK, doll, why don't you climb into bed? It's a big day tomorrow."

I did as I was told, pulling back the covers and slipping into my bed. Mom turned away slightly, a look of embarrassment on her face.

"I want to call Dad." I don't know why I said it, but my childish instincts told me to bring my father into that Houston motel room by any means necessary.

"What?" Mom laughed nervously. "It'd cost a fortune to call your dad from here."

"I don't care," I told her. "I really miss him. I wish he had come on this trip with us."

"Well, you know he had to work, doll. We'll be home in a few days."

I didn't want to confront her with my imaginings, but I looked right at her and said, "I just wish we could always be together."

The words hung in the air. Outside I could hear the call of a single bird on a nearby telephone pole. Mom seemed to be weighing the import of my challenge. Slowly, she came over and put her gentle hand against my face, brushing my hair into place. She kissed me on the cheek—twice.

"You know what, honey," she managed. "We always will be together. I promise."

"Really?"

"Uh-huh." She sat down on the edge of my bed and made slow little circles on my back with her hand. "For ever and ever and ever." There was a long, precious moment of unstated confession. "I guess sometimes when we travel around and put on shows and hear people are clapping for us, we get kind of silly. We forget that Waldo isn't real. But *you* are real—and I won't forget." I drifted off to sleep.

The next day in the limo, we sat in the back seat by ourselves. Mom by the window and me next to her.

Despite that chapter of drama, what still made our publicity tour to the Southwest worthwhile for me was that it had followed right on the heels of my most successful adventure as a part of the *Our Gang* circle. The evening Dad and I read through the script on our front porch, I knew I was going to be in a winner.

"Wow!" Dad had grinned as we got to the *fade to black* sign-off at the bottom of page twelve. "What a great story for you, kid!"

"I don't end up with Darla," I pointed out.

"Doesn't matter." He clapped me on the back, "You're the star of this one, bub." He tossed the stapled pages in the air. "And look at that scene you got on page five! That's what we in the biz call a 'soliloquy.'"

"Huh?"

Dad hugged me proudly. "A big speech. All eyes on Sir Waldo."

The story was essentially a redo of our 1934 hit *Hi'-Neighbor!*—substituting a boat race for the earlier contest with fire engines. Now entitled *Three Men in a Tub,* for once the romantic triangle had Alfalfa matching wits with me instead of with Butch. We filmed it in February of 1938, and the opening scenes have our feminine heroine missing. The gang is at a picnic, but Darla is ostensibly home minding the baby. News flash: she's actually with her new beau—yours truly! A frustrated Alfalfa is shocked when he looks out on the lake and sees his girlfriend gliding along in the back of my power yacht.

In the agony of jealousy, Alfalfa fails to be comforted when Spanky says to him, "Hey, what you need to give that smart-aleck Waldo is some competition."

"Why, I wouldn't give that guy *anything,*" he retorts.

Meanwhile, Darla is dreamy-eyed about both my love boat and me. "Your boat is divine!" she gushes, fluttering her eyelashes and nibbling daintily on the complimentary chocolates that I offered to all of my onboard guests. I stay right in character. "She's a very trim craft." When she asks me, I explain to Darla that things of beauty, grace, and speed are always referred to in the feminine gender. I still remember that the wardrobe department had outfitted me in a pair of expensive cream-colored slacks, a long-sleeved silk shirt with the sleeves fashionably rolled partway up my forearms, and a black necktie. They also gave me a pair of round horn-rimmed glasses that made me look a bit like the current Harry Potter.

The funniest part of the story is when little Porky and Buckwheat arrive at the dock with a message from Alfalfa. They get there in style, both of them astride Bessie, an old mare so swaybacked that their feet almost drag in the dirt. I still don't know where our producers found such a pathetic equine specimen. The boys walk over and chide Darla for leaving their club president in such an emotional lurch. "He feels terrible," Buckwheat laments.

Darla sniffs disdainfully. "I don't care if he does."

The messengers then deliver their ultimatum from Alfalfa. "If you think you're so smart, I challenge you to a boat race," the note reads.

My new sweetheart interjects that Alfalfa's "just being smart; he hasn't even got a boat." But I examine the message carefully and decide that my dignity and manhood have been highly offended. At this point, page five in the script, I begin to pace and then dramatically deliver the speech:

> In regards to this note, my good man, your illiterate friend conveys the idea of competing with me in a contest of speed by water. Please convey my compliments to Alfalfa and inform him that if he will abide by the rules of the Amateur Yachting Association, and race a craft seven feet W-L [I still don't know what that means] two foot beam, six inch shaft, maximum speed four knots, par as specified in *Lloyd's Book of Yacht Racing Regulations,* with any and all whereases and wherefores as recognized in British cruiser racing codes, I will accept his impertinent challenge, with a thorough understanding that the contest ends when one contestant has successfully negotiated one lap around the lake—is that clear?

I finish the speech with an intimidating step toward the two goggle-eyed boys, jabbing a finger toward them. Intimidated, they back away in awe. Buckwheat, gulping hard, gives a classic response: "Yes, sir, it's clear—only what am I going to tell Alfalfa?"

In his review of the episode, Leonard Maltin does a word count and then emphatically asserts that this has definitely got to be the longest single bit of dialogue in *Our Gang's* entire twenty-two-year history. I do know we weren't able to film the scene in the usual way. Normally, Gordon Douglas, in shooting dialogue, would get scenes a bit at a time. Most of the actors weren't good at memorizing; improvisations and malapropisms were tolerated and even encouraged. By using various camera angles and frequent cuts between them, no one usually had to have more than a couple of sentences in his or her head at a time. But this particular episode was piloted by newcomer director Nate Watt, who usually worked in town as an assistant director, a job he held on pictures such as *All Quiet on the Western Front* and *Of Mice and Men*. He wanted to get the entire response in one extended camera shot as I paced back and forth in front of my boat, so I dutifully memorized the entire 116-word speech. The finished product did have some cute cutaways of Buckwheat and Porky agog and mesmerized by my eloquence, but I can promise you we did it in one steady take.

Meanwhile, Alfalfa and company have been busy in the clubhouse, sawing and hammering to create their own mystery ship: *Darla the 4th*. The script has several moments that are quirky and nonsensical. Buckwheat walks in triumphantly carrying a baritone horn that is somehow necessary to this shipbuilding project. Spanky admires it but asks skeptically, "Did your father say you could have this?" Buckwheat flashes his characteristic smile. "It's OK—he's not home!"

The day of the race took the entire gang out on location. The race officially takes place at Toluca Lake, but in actuality we traveled to Malibu Lake instead. Some of the scenes in which Darla and I are in the boat had already been fake-shot with the process screen—and astute viewers probably noticed the bit of echo that was caused by being in a soundproofed tank of water in the studio. But to add realism, we also had a full day of real location shooting in the Santa Monica Mountains.

Anytime the show had to go on the road, a man named Bob Davis drove us there in a medium-size red bus that had the words "Our Gang Comedies" painted on the side in bold white letters. Mom had to go with us to Malibu Lake, and I remember her standing with some of the other moms in the shade of some big trees as we laboriously ground out the various boating scenes.

For the race itself, wardrobe had upgraded me to a sharp-looking blue double-breasted blazer, white pleated dress trousers, white shoes, and a jaunty racing cap. My spectacles are replaced by a pair of expensive racing goggles. Interestingly, all *Our Gang* films had a person who had just one assignment: keep track of conflicting details that might creep up between shots. Since filming a scene might spread out over several days, this person had to meticulously write down what each actor was wearing and whether each person's jacket was buttoned or unbuttoned. Did her scarf fold to the left or the right? Was he holding that book in his left or right hand the last time we left off? Audiences always delighted in catching Hollywood pros in a flub, and the continuity person or "script girl" was charged with making sure that didn't happen. In later years, such people took a mountain of Polaroid shots to record the unnoticed details of each scene; most recently, digital cameras are the tool of choice. But on the set of *Three Men in a Tub*, a newcomer named Ellen Corby hovered around, writing down what Darla, Alfalfa, and I were wearing. She was married to our photographer, Francis Corby, and later went on to have a successful acting career of her own, capping her years in the trade by playing the part of Granny in CBS's hit *The Waltons*.

There at the edge of the lake, Spanky pompously announces that Alfalfa has constructed this mystery craft at the cost of "thousands of dollars. Probably more!" A tarp is lifted to reveal a masked Alfalfa and his two crew members: Porky and Buckwheat.

I graciously applaud the introduction and call out rather sportingly,

"Well said, my good man." Darla and I climb into my power boat, and I offer her a small repast: yet another box of expensive candies. "Oh, Waldo, you're simply divine!" she gushes in a simpering voice as our two boats lurch forward from the starting line.

This story borrows from the familiar motif of animal power harnessed for *Our Gang* transportation. Clear back in 1923, Farina appeared in a two-reeler entitled *Back Stage*, in which the kids nailed together a two-story touring bus driven by donkey power. He would pull a string that dropped feed in front of the abused beast of burden. (A feather duster tickling the donkey into a *hee-haw* served as a horn.) Mules scrambling after carrots and dogs chasing cats provided similar locomotion in other film shorts. In our tale, Alfalfa's ragtag boat is fueled by a clever device: a turning wheel that drops floating feed pellets in front of three ravenous geese. In addition, Porky, stationed at the stern, has a black umbrella hoisted aloft, and he continually lifts a dampened finger to check wind currents so that he can adjust the angle and pitch of their homemade sail according to his mental trigonometry.

The race itself is anticlimactic; the lead seesaws back and forth, with Alfalfa hollering at Buckwheat to "give it all she's got!" He spins the feed wheel faster, ostensibly causing the geese to paddle with furious intensity. Darla wrings her hands and moans in female despair: "Oh, Waldo, they're gaining on us!" Each time I simply throttle up the engine, and we surge ahead, to the point where I almost pilot us right over an unmarked treacherous dam that has a thirty-foot drop.

"We haven't a thing to worry about," I gloat with nonchalant pride as we glide toward the finish line, with Darla continuing to bat her eyes at me. All at once, the yacht springs a leak and begins to founder. As Waldo, who is a man of all knowledge and no guts, I commence leafing through my technical owner's manual and reading aloud, "In case of accident, shut off the motor." Meanwhile, Darla, now a damsel in distress, cries out, "Oh, somebody save me! Please! Alfalfa!"

Peeling off his shirt, my rival dives into the water and paddles over to where we are doing a slow imitation of *Titanic*. Alfalfa picks Darla up, and as it turns out, is able to stand in what seems to be less than a foot and a half of water. Before the cameras rolled, Darla stoutly protested, "I don't want you to carry me. I'm afraid you'll drop me!" That gave our director a brainstorm, and he whispered into Alfalfa's ear that he should go ahead and "slip." They both tumble into the waves as I look into the camera, mournfully asking, "Now, how could that have happened?" On the shore, Buckwheat and Porky hold aloft a cork that they had somehow removed from the hull of my rapidly disappearing pleasure craft.

Oh well. You can get top billing or you can get the girl—but you can't usually get both at the same time.

Chapter Eight

MOVING TO
METRO-GOLDWYN-MAYER

A unique era was drawing to a close, but at the time, none of us knew it.

As I said earlier, Hal Roach was a uniquely gifted man who loved children and made our lives as happy and carefree as possible under the harsh glare of the media spotlight. We were well paid, protected, and pampered. And directors like Gordon Douglas knew just how to get the best out of each performer. Many years later, Spanky reminisced with friends about how Douglas would stand up in the center of the group of kids and explain the story, acting it out with the gestures and screen tricks he had in mind. He would encourage an actor who wasn't quite getting the nuance of a story or scene, and he never scolded.

"[Gordon] was one of the best directors I ever worked with," Tommy "Butch" Bond wrote in his autobiography. "I didn't work for him, I worked *with* him. He would get down on his knees to be at eye level. Being younger than some of my other directors probably gave him an insight into how kids felt. I could sink my teeth into the part because I had real direction. . . . He was compassionate. He had moxie and drive, and he could get talent out of kids. He worked on each of us. That's what inaugurated the golden age of the *Gang*."[1]

As I've said, I feel hugely fortunate to have been in the series during its heyday. Alfalfa, Spanky, Buckwheat, Butch, and Darla were the finest cast Hal Roach ever assembled, and I was lucky to be at least on the periphery of this pinnacle. Out of thousands who tried out, exactly 176 children ever acted in the series, and I got to be with this top-rated team. Leonard Maltin said as much when he observed, "There's little doubt *Our Gang*'s finest years are represented by the Roach sound films from mid-1930s through 1937. . . . Hal Roach says that Cary Grant, while he was on the lot making the first *Topper* film, 'used to sit and watch *Our Gang* for half an hour at a time, marveling at their ability to convey an idea even though they were such little kids. He was amazed at how convincing they could be.' "[2] To my chagrin I missed, by less than a year, being in the franchise's only Oscar-winning film: *Bored of Education* was the Academy's pick for best short subject in 1936.

And these whiz kids were my on- and off-screen playmates!

It's stunning to realize that a hugely talented kid named Mickey Rooney traveled with his mom all the way to Hollywood specifically for the purpose of trying to break into *Our Gang*. He didn't make it. Part of the reason was that he was one of those overpainted prodigies whose affected airs in screen tests were a turnoff for our visionary Hal Roach. " 'To my mind,' " he revealed later, " [Rooney] was acting more like an adult than a kid. He was a very good little actor, and maybe somebody could have worked on him to tone him down, but that was also work.' "[3]

The other startling rejection for the franchise was a bubbling tot named Shirley Temple, whose ambitious mother actually brought her to Culver City, not once, but five or six times. "She just never got beyond the outer office," Roach was to later tell his friends.

Somehow the casting director never saw what he was looking for; and, as Roach remembers it, the outer office was generally swamped with a great number of pushy mothers with their overcoached offspring in tow.

Leonard Maltin analyzes the roadblocks to *Our Gang* stardom: "The studio would receive close to a thousand pictures from hopeful parents every month, while hundreds more would try to crash the studio gates. Studio statistics showed that approximately 10 percent of all these moppets would win studio interviews. Less than 5 percent of *those* kids would get as far as Hal Roach's office. A screen test followed only for those most exceptional aspirants, and many more failed than passed this test. Each year perhaps four or five candidates would be given single picture 'extra' contracts, but only one or two might have that special chemistry to become full-fledged *Our Gang*ers."[4] Even after getting to the inner circle, it was understood in Culver City that a newbie was essentially on probation for the first three months, just to see if he or she could get used to the harsh lights and the intense adult world of hard work and grueling schedules. Every now and then, a child would simply not be able to overcome camera jitters and would wash out of the gig.

It was a challenging gauntlet out there, and I honestly have to give God the credit for the fact that somehow I landed in this amazing talent pool—and inherited such an unconventional conversion story.

As early as 1936, industry people could tell, though, that the day of the movie short was numbered. For one simple reason: America was turning toward the double feature. People on Great Depression budgets expected to see two films for the price of one—a current hit and then also a second bill or B movie. With that trend sweeping across the nation, there wasn't nearly as much of a need for cartoons, newsreels, and things like *Our Gang* shorts to round out a fun evening at the theater.

Already Roach had begun to face up to this new paradigm by making the most of our movies' one-reel stories, which happened in a brisk ten minutes. In some of the shows in which I had a part, reviewers marveled at how our storytelling team could set up a complicated plot plus jokes and then deliver the entire package in just that one reel. *The Pigskin Palooka* was a 1937 football tale in which I had one skimpy scene taking a photo of Alfalfa, but the clever script told an intricate sports story, replete with sight gags, players slipping on banana peels, a lot of gridiron action, and it clocked in at exactly 10 minutes 12 seconds. But by the time we got to the 1938 season, our beloved owner, Mr. Roach, could read the handwriting on the wall. Already Laurel and Hardy were a thing of the past, and Roach was setting his sights on getting into feature films himself, correctly sensing that they were the cinematic wave of the future.

I didn't know it at the time, but when a studio messenger boy delivered *Came the Brawn* to Mom and me one Friday afternoon, it was the last movie I would ever make for Hal Roach Studios. And what a winner! I had a big part in this boxing saga, and when I got the final page, I gave a whoop of triumph! "I get her! I get her!"

"What?" Mom teasingly reached for the pages. "You get who?"

She knew very well who. I'd stood on the sidelines while Alfalfa and Butch vied for the heart of the lovely Darla Hood. And, of course, I had gone down with the ship while my lady love fell into Alfalfa's arms at the end of our Toluca Lake boat race. But finally, Mr. Roach had kept the promise he made to Dad and me in my job interview. It was going to be my turn.

Actually, there's a small secret I can share now. Despite what movie audiences were seeing up on the screen, little Darla had been edging in my direction all summer long.

I'll be the first to say that it was innocent kid stuff. But on a couple of occasions, Mom had taken the initiative and had invited Darla over to our house. We went to the Los Angeles County Fair together once, just the three of us, and spent a day of delirious fun on the merry-go-rounds and pony rides. I wore a hat pulled low over my eyes, and Darla had on some kiddie dark glasses and a red bonnet; nobody recognized us. And there was this incredible pizza parlor about four blocks away from our house; sometimes our two families would go there on a Saturday night and stuff ourselves silly in a secluded corner booth.

Came the Brawn gave several of us a chance to shine, but, as usual, the story played off of a Spanky brainchild. There was really no one else like our own George McFarland. He got the nickname Spanky because, as a toddler, he was forever getting into mischief. His exasperated mom continually barked at him, "Spank-ee, spank-ee, mustn't touch." Born in Dallas, he was already doing agency modeling for still photos at the age of three when an ambitious aunt of his mailed some mug shots out to the Hal Roach Studios. When he came to California for a screen test, everyone on the lot was instantly agog. "You've got to come see this kid!" James Horne, the cinematographer told them. "He explodes with charisma!" Spanky was immediately given a role in the current story, *Free Eats,* and stayed in Culver City for the next ten years, graduating quickly to a hundred dollar weekly paycheck. He delivered hilarious gag lines with an amazingly innocent straight face. In a top-rated adventure *The Kid From Borneo,* he's afraid that a visiting sideshow entertainer is actually a cannibal. Afraid for his life, he informs the ravenous visitor: "I don't think I'll taste so good. Mom says I'm spoiled."

It's hard to believe, but innocent toddlers such as Spanky and Darla honestly didn't realize they were making movies! Both of them confessed later that, as far as they could tell, they were playing in a dirt lot where there happened to be lots of lights around. " 'It was like living in a dream world,' " Darla related. " 'They just kept telling me,

I agree (under duress) to throw a wrestling match. Already Hollywood is corrupting my morals.

well, do this and that, and I thought I was sort of performing just for them. I didn't understand what a motion picture camera was, or what it was doing in the way of recording my actions.' "[5]

As a three-year-old, Spanky was seemingly unconscious of the camera. He added in a later interview: " 'I was making pictures before my memory process started, and before I could walk. It was the only way of life I knew. For a long, long time I thought every kid grew up making pictures. Before adolescence, I really didn't think too much about being in the movies. I was actually eight or nine years old before I realized all kids *weren't* in the movies, and I never had any friends other than the gang. It wasn't like a job—but it wasn't exactly like playing either.' "[6] He told once how in 1935 a magazine interviewer asked him how old he was. "Six," he replied. "And how long have you been working in motion pictures?" the reporter wanted to know. "Seven years."

So by the time we got ready to film *Came the Brawn*, both Spanky and Darla were seasoned, unflappable professionals who knew their way around a studio shoot. The story begins with Spanky once again promoting a moneymaker: a wrestling title bout between Alfalfa, the "Oklahoma Wildcat," and well, whoever. Alfalfa wants this rigged match to be against somebody he can beat, but no one can decide who that might be. Spanky has lined up three wimp candidates; Alfalfa's afraid of all of them. For a little while, they think tiny Porky is a good candidate, but in a trial run, even Porky pins the Wildcat in just a few seconds.

Cue Waldo! Wearing my double-breasted navy Waldo blazer and with my fragile spectacles again, I happen to walk through the neighborhood with my nose in a book of Shakespeare. "Friends, Romans, countrymen, lend me your ears . . ." Instantly, the plan crystallizes. Surely Alfalfa can whip a milquetoast like Waldo! I'm amenable to the idea of taking a dive for a good cause, and the fix is in place. Alfalfa, confident in his eventual success, begins to crow and preen about the upcoming match and tells Darla he's about to be "champeen" of the world.

As usually happens in cases like this, pride goes before a fall. The day of the match, Butch and the Woim hijack the story in a back room. They make me surrender my Masked Marvel wrestling outfit to them—along with several pounds of tissue paper I used to boost my nonexistent pecs—and Butch takes my place in the ring. The ensuing story has a lot of great comedy, crowds shrieking, and the eternal duo of Buckwheat and Porky poking through the canvas with bolt cutters, which they use to separate Butch from his pants! Diving under the canvas to protect his modesty, he refuses to emerge, and Alfalfa is declared the winner by default.

So how does that help me ride off into the sunset with the fair damsel? In a remarkable twist of fate, the beautiful Darla is turned off by the over-the-top violence in the ring (even back then wrestling was fake) and decides she doesn't care much for either Butch or Alfalfa. Instead, she's seated in the crowd next to Waldo, who woos her by reading the heart-melting line from *Romeo and Juliet*: "Oh, that I were a glove upon that hand, that I might touch that cheek!" Even the Woim is moved to tears by the pathos and power of the immortal bard's words, and Darla, I'm pleased to say, is putty in my hands. She scornfully says to Alfalfa: "*I* like boys of refinement."

See, that's what I'd been trying to tell everyone for the past year.

The film ends with a rare shattering of cinematic spell. Alfalfa, crushed, declares in abject sorrow: "To think she'd do this to me—I'll never speak to another girl again as long as I live." And then looking right into the camera, he grimaces and adds, "Good night, folks." One reviewer, charmed, called it a "breaking of the fourth wall."

As *Brawn* hit the theater circuit and got booked on ten thousand screens that summer, I was feeling much better about life. Darla was flirting with me. I wasn't yet in Alfalfa's league in terms of acting or star power, but I was certainly on the fringes of great success.

One more thing had quietly been nudging me in a better direction as well. For most of the summer, I had finally started attending church.

It seemed that ever since I got my big break in *Glove Taps*, Pastor Kite had been praying harder than ever for his grandson. Oh, he never told me that, even though in reflecting back, I have the impression that he began writing to me with heightened regularity. Every couple of weeks I would get either a letter or a postcard from Nebraska, filled with news and bits of encouragement.

He never once said, "Hey, get yourself out of bed this Sabbath and go to church." But even though I was only eight, somehow the idea came to me. It wasn't a clear or coherent thought but more of a quiet impression, fueled, no doubt, by my earlier brush with the law. God was telling me, in maybe the only way He could reach me, that He had plans for my life.

After the shoplifting mess at Thanksgiving, I resolutely stayed away from that gang of kids who prowled our neighborhood. If I saw they were outside, I simply stayed home. I knew the park they liked to hang out in, and I just didn't go there any longer. Early 1938 had me spending free time with my tap lessons or an occasional outing with Alfalfa or Darla (never at the same time, obviously!).

A new family moved into the house on the corner around that time, and I soon became acquainted with them. His parents spoke with just a trace of an accent, but Carmelo had been born in San Diego and chattered away in perfect English. He was about a year younger than I was and was hugely enamored of my success in films. I took him to see *Hearts Are Thumps,* which was still playing locally, and he kept pointing at the screen. "I can't believe it; I can't believe it," he repeated over and over. "That's you, man. This is so cool." Obviously I enjoyed his company!

His mother cooked enormous, exotic meals, which left me staggering from the table whenever I got to stay for dinner. "Oh, have just a little more," she would press, ladling creamy puddings into my bowl. They took me with them to the beach one Sunday and paid for us to rent bikes and ride along the long wooden pier.

I knew that every Sunday morning, they attended a church over in Burbank, and I was pleased when they invited me to attend with them. I asked Mom and Dad, and they both shrugged their acceptance.

Sunday School at Carmelo's church was disorganized but fun, with a couple of twin sisters in their twenties who taught us songs and gave the kids all kinds of pictures to cut out. When they realized that I was a "big film star," as Carmelo boasted to them, their eyes glowed. "You've got to help us with VBS!" I had no idea what those letters stood for, but when they explained that each summer they put on crafts and Bible plays for the neighborhood children, I eagerly agreed. All summer long I was King Joseph, then Moses, and even the apostle Peter who denied Jesus three times. Some of the local parents even came to watch our Vacation Bible School productions, and I could see them nudging and pointing as they recognized me from *Came the Brawn*. A couple of times parents even asked me for autographs, and I blushed and signed a potluck napkin or church bulletin for them.

Being at church week by week was giving me the chance to slowly form my own spiritual beliefs, sometimes melded together with the gentle doses of generic faith that we encountered on the set. Occasionally during our work breaks, we would get to watch some of the classic reruns from earlier years, especially if we were working on a remake of a certain episode. The guys and I saw one going back to 1932, in which Stymie is trying to rescue his beloved dog, Pete, from being put to sleep by a villainous dogcatcher who is demanding payment of a five-dollar fine. He prays earnestly to the Lord for help, tearfully telling God, "Pete's the onliest friend I got in this world." *Instantly* he's rewarded by having a divine gust of wind blow a five-dollar bill right into his face. Looking to heaven in devoted praise, he rejoices, "Man, now that's what I call service!" I still wasn't brave enough to openly say my own prayers before dinner, or especially in the Our Gang Café, but sometimes before dropping off to sleep I would murmur some of my stray preadolescent thoughts to the Lord.

Summer was drawing to a close when *Our Gang* was hit with a stunning headline. We were being sold to MGM! Hal Roach was no longer going to be the owner and mentor of this franchise.

In one way, it didn't seem that this would be a huge disruption to the *Gang*. Beginning in 1922, Roach had chosen a company called Pathé Exchange to be his distributor. They marketed silent films around the country under the well-known logo of a rooster. But just five years into the deal, Roach decided the grass was greener over on the MGM side of the fence, so he was already using Metro-Goldwyn-Mayer as his distributor. Now, eleven wildly successful years later, he was actually selling *Our Gang* to MGM and walking away a multi-millionaire. As World War II got underway, he allowed the air force to essentially camp out in his Culver City film lot and make promotional films with a young actor named Ronald Reagan.

But why did he choose to sell *Our Gang*?

Several reasons were being openly discussed in the gossip on and off the set. As I mentioned earlier, double features were threatening to drive the short film market out of business entirely. Roach possibly saw the demise of his beloved pet project, and wanted to get out before the ship foundered.

In addition, it was getting more and more expensive to make *Our Gang* comedies and still turn a profit. I know they weren't paying Waldo a whole lot more, but all production costs were escalating rapidly, and it was a competitive business. Profit margins were getting smaller all the time.

Probably the dagger that struck home was the tightening market monopoly by a few large players. From the beginning, theaters around the country rented the films they wanted to show, and business was thriving. For years, it was easy for Hal Roach to send out the word that a new *Our Gang* episode was on its way, and everybody signed up. Film reviewers were perennially bragging about Roach comedies, and Hollywood newsletters contained studio ads that boasted, "If you had to pay per laugh, you'd pay feature prices for these comedies!" One rag sheet informed theater owners, "Many theaters are billing [these shorts] *above* the feature." When *Beginner's Luck,* Alfalfa's first film, was released in 1935, the industry magazine *Film Daily* shouted its approval, "If you don't play it up in marquee lights, you shouldn't own a marquee." Rental dollars flowed in, and the free market was making Mr. Roach extremely wealthy.

However, by 1938, more and more studios were doing something called "block booking." A major company such as Paramount or MGM would release a spectacular new feature film and securely tie it to their own chosen comedy short or newsreel. For example, any theater wanting to show *You Can't Take It With You* or Spencer Tracy's new film *Boys Town* or the James Cagney crime drama *Angels With Dirty Faces* had to also agree to rent the shorts and newsreels those blockbuster studios had put with the main feature. It became an all-or-nothing package, and this new reality was slowly squeezing Hal Roach in the pocketbook. All these years, he had been a producer not a distributor. Not being a serious player in the features scene, it was increasingly a challenge for him to get large theater chains to take an independent *Our Gang* comedy, even one that ran a modest ten minutes.

MGM, on the other hand, made full-length films all the time and was well positioned to do its own block booking with Alfalfa's continuing adventures. So the deal was struck and quickly announced in *Variety.* In a poignant moment of irony, Alfalfa came out right at the end of *Hide and Shriek,* Roach's last *Our Gang* picture, and wordlessly hung a sign on the door: Out of Bizzness.

Was this going to be the end of Waldo's career? Mom and Dad, who gratefully cashed my paycheck every Friday afternoon at the bank, were anxiously wondering about that. And even as the first flickers of my spiritual self began to emerge, I had some questions for God myself.

Chapter Nine

BLACK AND WHITE IN THE MOVIES

They say one sometimes finds God's signals in the strangest places, and almost the moment we *Our Gang* kids arrived at MGM, a divine message was embedded in the very first screenplay we read. It was a new experience being on the Metro-Goldwyn-Mayer film lots; back then MGM was the largest studio in the world. All of us were pleased to see that Gordon Douglas was still there to be our director, and *The Little Ranger* seemed to be yet another high-quality story with the usual high jinks.

Unfortunately, I had to reluctantly turn Darla back over to the usual Alfalfa versus Butch franchise rivalry. As the story opens, Alfalfa is loitering outside a movie theater for his girl, only to blanch when she arrives on the arm of his rival. Crushed, he goes in to watch a cowboy western starring "Fearless Bill." I remember sitting right behind Butch and Darla as the opening credits roll.

Alfalfa dozes off there in the theater and drifts into a weird and wonderful dreamland where all of the *Our Gang* members are suddenly stars in the shoot-'em-up. He's the hero, Butch is the villain, Buckwheat and Porky are sheriffs leading the posse, and there's a keg of TNT dynamite about to explode. And me? Get this: part of the dream sequence has an old-time revival preacher in the action, and there I am with a Bible and a rugged western town to save.

Now, I'm not about to say God directly inspired that bit of cinematic "prophecy." The story, by the way, was crafted by a talented Hal Law and *Our Gang*'s first director, Bob McGowan. But decades later, as I stood in the pulpit and preached for real, I will concede that I had occasional flashbacks!

Another point of interest is that *The Little Ranger* had an internal "working title," which was common in that era. There on the MGM set, Alfalfa's exploits as a gunslinger were sardonically dubbed *Gun With the Wind*. The reason for that title will become clear as the chapter continues.

We had barely wiped the makeup and gunpowder residue off our faces when our new bosses corralled us for yet another film, this one dubbed *Party Fever*. To this day, there is an annual Strawberry Festival in Ventura, California, and that leads to a clever plot setup. I get to ask Darla to go with me to the event, but she demurely tells me that both Butch and Alfalfa have already invited her and are about to come to blows.

Ever the diplomat, Waldo suggests a solution. The story introduces a pompous-looking character named Uncle Frank, played by Frank Jaquet, who was invariably typecast as a lawyer or politician. (He capped off a long career of mostly bit parts, by acting in the classic O. Henry tale, *The Gift of the Magi*, in 1952's *O. Henry's Full House*.) The town is getting ready to celebrate Boys' Week, with Jaquet as mayor, proposing to appoint a "junior mayor" as part of the civics lesson. Why not let Alfalfa and Butch vie for that honor, with the winner getting to take Darla to the Strawberry Festival as an additional prize? Both boys agree, and they launch into a ferocious political extravaganza that would put today's presidential campaigns to shame. Butch offers his supporters a free marshmallow roast, only to

We're in our new digs over at MGM, and Alfalfa and Butch are sparring over Darla yet again. But I win the Strawberry Festival contest—and Darla—with the help of Uncle Frank, who happens to be the mayor and judge!

be outdone by Alfalfa's hiring a skywriting balloon in order to attract a crowd.

So who wins the gavel and the pretty girl? When it's time to make a choice, the mayor rejects both candidates for their cheap stunts, reminding the crowd: "Honesty and faithful service will always win out over sensationalism." With that, he gives the keys to the city—to *me*! According to him, I had written the best student essay on the virtues of good government—and of course, essays by Waldo are typed, double-spaced, and without misspelled words. True to the enduring reality of movie nepotism, I give away the secret when I blurt out to the mayor: "Thanks, Uncle Frank!"

One interesting surprise was that MGM abruptly sprung a new

director on us. A baby-faced kid named George Sidney, barely twenty-one, was sent in to pilot the second comedy for the studio's new franchise. He never let on that he was only a few years older than our senior *Our Gang* cast member, Alfalfa's older brother, Harold. He was a stickler for detail, and did a fine job of putting us through our paces. Years later I heard that he had gone on to direct such big features as *Annie Get Your Gun, Show Boat, Bye Bye Birdie,* and a musical called *Viva Las Vegas* with a hot acting sensation from Tennessee named Elvis Presley.

One day, not long after this, as Dad and I were walking off the set and heading to the car, my agent stopped us with a fascinating offer. "You're right here at MGM anyway," he explained, "and they're getting ready to do maybe the biggest movie of all time."

"What's it called?" Dad paused to consider the opportunity.

Mr. Sherril held out a studio blurb. "Negotiations have already been underway for a couple of years, I hear. David Selznick just coughed up fifty grand for the option to Margaret Mitchell's novel—don't know if you read it—called *Gone With the Wind.*"

Dad shook his head. "Didn't get around to it. I hear it sold a bunch of copies."

"Oh, huge. It's a sweeping Civil War story, and should fill up the screen like you wouldn't believe."

My father grinned. "And, of course, they want Darwood here to play the lead role."

A short laugh, then a pause as Lew fumbled in his pockets for a cigarette. He lit it and shook his head. "Nah. But they tell me MGM is going to have a cast of thousands, and there will be lots of days where extras can pick up a few bucks." He put a friendly hand on my shoulder. "Sorry, kid. I wish there was something bigger. But at least it'd go on your résumé that you were in the biggest film ever."

It was after the first of the year, in early 1939, before MGM began shooting. As things turned out, I ended up being in just one scene: a fiery moment when people are fleeing the devastation of Atlanta as the Civil War grinds to a tragic conclusion. There were a couple of moments, though, when I chanced to walk past as Clark Gable and Vivien Leigh were filming their memorable scenes. Truth be told, years later when I watched *Gone With the Wind* on video, my own screen presence was so minuscule that I honestly couldn't spot myself in the saga. But after spending so much time in grainy black-and-white shorts running ten minutes, it was exciting to have any part at all in a full-color, widescreen spectacle that filled up three spellbinding hours of Technicolor drama.

Once again, a blockbuster opportunity like this illustrates that, in Hollywood, it's invariably whom you know that counts. Back in 1935, a couple of years before I got my big break, *Our Gang* did a show called *Anniversary Trouble,* and needed a character actress to play a maid. I'm told kids on the set had a great time with "Mandy," a large-hearted—actually she was rather large all over—African-American star who stole the show as Buckwheat's mother. Now, as the casting people for *Gone With the Wind* were filling the various roles, they turned again to Hattie McDaniel to play the substantial part of Mammy. She had an MGM connection already through *Our Gang,* and had appeared in *China Seas* with Gable, a friendship that helped her get into *Gone With the Wind.* She did such a brilliant job that she won the Best Supporting Actress Award for 1940, the first black star to achieve such an honor. Interestingly, she beat out Eleanor Roosevelt's personal maid, Elizabeth McDuffie, for the part. (No pressure, mind you.)

Which brings to the fore a reality that had always been a part of Hollywood's checkered history—and *Our Gang's* as well. We were part of a politically progressive community, and yet, it is tragically true that the film stories we told had their own disturbing elements of racial prejudice. There was fierce criticism for the sometimes placid, unrealistic way slavery was presented in the sanitized splendor of *Gone With the Wind*. Columnist and critic Leonard Pitts was scathing in calling the picture "a romance set in Auschwitz." McDaniel and others, it was suggested, were guilty of portraying the "happy slave," content to serve others and sing or dance their way through life. On the other hand, the role of Prissy in the film seemed to typify the black character, too often stupid and childlike, willing to be led around by others. There was a devastating scene in the movie in which actress Butterfly McQueen screams hysterically, "Lawzy, we got to have a doctor. I don't know nothin' 'bout birthin' babies!" Scarlett slaps her in the face, and for the next decade, McQueen was unable to get any roles in Hollywood that went beyond that demeaning characterization.

How was it on the set of *Our Gang*? We have to remember that these comedy shorts were filmed during the 1920s and 1930s when the racial climate was much different from today. Three main African-American characters dominated during that period: Allen Clayton "Farina" Hoskins, Matthew "Stymie" Beard Jr., and then my friend and coactor, William "Buckwheat" Thomas Jr. All three were brilliant character actors, precocious, funny, articulate performers—and I'll be the first to say that they outshone me in charisma and acting ability many times over. One odd tidbit is that both Farina and Buckwheat occasionally were portrayed in female roles; Farina actually wore a dress a couple of times. But as their fame grew, *Our Gang* eventually placed them firmly and permanently on the boy side of our Culver City campus. Farina, the moment he left Hollywood, immediately grew a mustache to proudly affirm his resolute maleness—and kept it the rest of his life! He had a fine career as an adult, working with handicapped kids. "Give me the rejects," he once told questioners. "I can work with people who are nobodies. I love these people." Sidney Poitier was later instrumental in getting the deserving comic genius into the Black Filmmakers Hall of Fame. For my money, Farina and Jackie Cooper shared one of the wittiest bits of repartee in *Our Gang* history, when 1931's *Love Business* has Cooper falling head over heels for the beautiful Miss Crabtree. Farina opines, "You're just lovesick, that's all." An enthralled Jackie confesses, "I'm a whole epidemic!"

Stymie came to *Our Gang* in 1930 and debuted in the classic *Teacher's Pet,* one of our best five-star productions, also holding his own with the incomparable Cooper. He was five years old at the time, and his father, a pastor in downtown Los Angeles, had heard through the grapevine that Roach was auditioning black kids to replace the aging Farina. The duo arrived at the studio where three hundred fifty kids had already shown up to try out for the part. Bob McGowan took one look at this child's face and immediately blurted, "Him! That's the one I want." They gave him a five-year contract on the spot, no screen test required.

Bob McGowan, though, soon discovered that his latest find, while a clever actor, was forever bumping into props and getting in the way. He sighed to a friend, "He's beautiful, but, man, that kid stymies me all the time!" Forever after that, Stymie was his name. He wore a trademark derby in every episode—a prop borrowed from his hero, Stan Laurel—and while other children were "in makeup," he had his head shaved smooth each week by the studio's in-house barber.

" 'They used to call me "One-take Stymie," ' " he said later. " 'I didn't burn up too much film, and I'm very proud of that. But it all just came natural, like most kids five, six, seven years old, I wasn't too aware. A lot of my ability just came from the natural thing, that I guess was a gift from the Good Lord.' "[1] According to other *Our Gang* members, Stymie's family was the only one that often invited the others over for parties and ice-cream socials.

As I mentioned before, the comedies cheerfully dealt with the reality that while Spanky and Alfalfa were going to experience measles with dark spots on their light skin, Buckwheat got the "white measles"—just so they would show. Spanky, ordered to wash his face in one episode, says to Buckwheat, "You're lucky!" Back in Farina's day, when filming a scary tale called *Shivering Spooks,* Mary Kornman begins reading a ghost story to the other kids. Farina pops up with a fair question: "Hey, how come there's only *white* ghosts?" Mary gives a logical answer. "Colored people can't be ghosts. How could you see them in the dark?" Unfazed and unoffended, Farina reasons, "They could carry lanterns, couldn't they?"[2] So that lighthearted exchange reads as innocent fun even today, but a year earlier, Farina was in a tale entitled *Your Own Back Yard,* interestingly enough with a girl named Fay Wray, later the star in 1933's *King Kong.* The ad blurb read as follows: "Farina, dusky juvenile of *Our Gang,* is very lonesome and wants to play with the white boys, but is rebuffed continually. Mammy tells him to stay in his 'own back yard.' " Viewers today are rightly outraged at such expressions. As Farina grew to be a star, studio blurbs referred to him as "that chocolate-coated fun drop of Hal Roach's Rascals."

In *General Spanky,* which was *Our Gang*'s only attempt at a feature-length production, the Civil War setting is replete with a number of offensive characterizations. It often refers to slave masters and to black children as pickaninnies. Buckwheat, who gets lost, realizes that for self-preservation he had better latch on to General Spanky; any unattached slave "is likely to be shot."

I appreciate the positive reality that society looks back today with a heightened sense of conscience. When the *Our Gang* shorts began to make their way to television in the early 1950s, now dubbed *The Little Rascals,* a number of episodes were trimmed to eliminate offending material. Some twenty-minute shows got sliced down to ten because of tacky dialogue or insensitive scenes; others have frankly never been shown on-air because of the slowly changing mores of society. Wisely, TV executives invited civil-rights groups such as the National Association for the Advancement of Colored People (NAACP) to help review the stories and edit them to make them acceptable to the improved standards of the mid-twentieth century.

The reality in 1937, though, is that we worked and played together in Hal Roach's fantasy world in full harmony. Some moviegoers in the Deep South protested the fact that *Our Gang* showed white kids and black kids attending school together; our standard retort was that even on the set, we were all in one color-blind classroom. "I've looked at the scrapbooks," Spanky observed much later. "There's me, Stymie, the bulldog, and Alfalfa going to school together in 1935, the first integrated classroom in the country."

I was privileged to work with Buckwheat, and even as a small child, he carried himself with dignity and style. There was nothing second-class about his work or about the challenging roles he portrayed with such finesse and charm.

Hal Roach, who lived to be one hundred and appreciated the growing racial sensitivity of the film industry, commented, " 'No one understands ethnic humor today, and . . . no one understands that there was never a malicious intent in any of this kind of comedy at the time it was made. I mean what's funny is funny, whether it's white or colored or whatever it is.' "[3] And, it was pointed out that *Our Gang* cheerfully had stereotypical categories for all sorts of kids: the freckled one, the bully, the really big kid, and so forth. I should know—Waldo was the first unabashed nerd out there, decades before Hollywood began penning "revenge" screenplays for us.

But the hard reality is that none of the rest of us could truly understand the unspoken and internal angst of these gifted African-American performers who sometimes had to wrestle with demeaning but lucrative opportunities. Two years after I left the series, Buckwheat had to act in *Unexpected Riches,* which had him riding through the black part of town in the back seat of a limousine, dispensing slices of watermelon and fried chicken to all takers. His predecessor, Farina, once did a story entitled *Spook Spoofing,* which used every tasteless racial cliché in the book.

It was back in 1930, nearly a decade before the sweeping injustices included in Scarlett O'Hara's love tale, when *Our Gang* briefly employed a razor-sharp comedian named Lincoln Perry for a two-reel comedy story entitled *A Tough Winter.* He was an educated and urbane performer who made a good living writing for a major newspaper but could also act in any variety of roles.

As history records it though, the *Our Gang* story helped him launch an ongoing character he dubbed "Stepin Fetchit," the idea being that he was so obsequious and mumbling that white people were always demanding that he "step and fetch it" for them. In our film and a number of others, Fetchit was a demeaning portrayal of black men who would shuffle along in ignorance, fulfilling the stereotype of being servile, shiftless, and simpleminded.

Perry, of course, was able to rationalize that his Fetchit character was sometimes *cunningly* dim-witted, and thus able to outfox his clumsy adversaries, a device borrowed handsomely by our own Buckwheat. In addition, this highly educated professional saw an opportunity to both exploit the racial atmosphere of the day for huge financial gain—he became the first African-American millionaire actor—and also paved the way for other black artists to eventually move into mainstream stardom. Farina, we found out later, finished his career with Roach, earning an eye-popping three hundred fifty dollars a week, many times what the other regulars were getting, and he was easily worth every penny.

Even Hattie McDaniel, in the aftermath of *Gone With the Wind,* was said to observe in her winsomely plainspoken way about the reality of being typecast in a role like Mammy, "Why should I complain about making seven hundred dollars a week playing a maid? If I didn't, I'd be making seven dollars a week actually being one." She was a pragmatic artist who accepted the challenge of slowly working to change the world in which she lived. When *Gone With the Wind* premiered in Atlanta in December of 1939, the city was seized by excitement. Unfortunately, local segregation laws dictated that if McDaniel attended the gala festivities, she would have to sit in the colored section of the film balcony. Not wanting to create a stir, she wrote to Selznick and graciously allowed that her schedule just then didn't permit her to make the trip. Clark Gable was so incensed by the unfairness of the situation that he threatened to boycott as well, until Hattie quietly urged him to go ahead and attend.

I look back now from the safe harbor of these many decades removed and remember moments that to Waldo seemed perfectly innocent, but which probably caused deep wounds to these friends of mine. Even now, Hollywood continues to wrestle with its cinematic demons of racial undercurrents. Black artists are too often relegated to secondary roles; African-American screen couples are rarely invited to play the lead roles in romantic stories. Asian performers struggle with the studios' jaded tendency to perennially cast them as the house boy or as members of knife-wielding street gangs.

And I reflect on how even, for society at large, racial divisions still are used to separate us and create false walls of suspicion. Certainly one of the key points I want to make in sharing my own *Our Gang* experiences is that these incredible artists did something unique I can never fully grasp. They wisely and winsomely balanced the realities of their own day with their deeply cherished vision of a better tomorrow.

In 1 Corinthians 7, Paul writes a gracious note to the Buckwheats and Hattie McDaniels of his era. Prejudice and unfairness are a stain belonging to every age, and it was present in the infant church. Slavery was part of the Roman culture, and some of those who worshiped with Paul and Silas were held in bondage.

His timeless counsel to them? Here it is, "Were you a slave when you were called [to the gospel]? Don't let it trouble you—although if you can gain your freedom, do so" (verse 21, NIV).

So there were hard moments in celluloid fantasy and also in real life when these courageous actors and actresses had to learn their lines and play a hard part. But there are other challenging moments in later times, when people like me, standing in pulpits, are called to speak for freedom and to pointedly condemn bigotry in all its poisonous manifestations. The Bible has a word of hope for Buckwheat and a word of responsibility for the grown-up Waldo.

Amen.

Chapter Ten

HOLLYWOOD'S FAST LANE

In our line of work, beautiful actresses would plaintively lament, "The clock's ticking!" Meaning two things, no doubt. First, as in every age, would the years continue to pass without a Prince Charming to come along? There were plenty of them milling around the studio, but finding the right guy then was as hard as it is now. Second, everyone from casting directors to agents knew that there were literally thousands of new beauties arriving in Southern California every year, each hoping to be the new Vivien Leigh or Darla Hood. Every wrinkle or gray hair was a stark reminder that time was running out.

In my case, the *Our Gang* countdown was simple—I was a rapidly maturing nine-year-old, and this was a franchise where only kids were allowed.

It was getting to be a stark reality; in 1939, Buckwheat was eight, Spanky was a creaky ten and a half, and Alfalfa was positively ancient at twelve. Even worse, Butch was nearing his thirteenth birthday, and there was open talk around MGM of having to push him out the door. Even little Darla was almost eight, and not nearly as perky and cute as before. Years later, Stymie was quoted as saying, " 'I heard the footsteps, but I didn't want to go.' "[1]

Two other realities began to refocus the picture. On the Hal Roach set, acting was hardly even work, except for having to endure Alfalfa's high jinks. Roach had been an affable boss, and we had enjoyed a hometown, convivial atmosphere. Now in the demanding world of Hollywood's most prestigious and successful studio, there was an unstated rule: *Stop kidding around. This is serious business, boys and girls.*

Asked about it later, an adult Darla Hood recalled a definite shift in the ambience when we left Hal Roach's kingdom and moved to MGM.

> "When we moved over to M-G-M, we knew something had changed, I mean even the kids felt it, and I remember Spanky and Alfalfa particularly sensed it. Instead of playing, having fun under a director's supervision, as we'd done back at the Roach lot, we suddenly became aware that we were supposed to be performing. After a few M-G-M shorts, I knew what I was doing, I knew I was acting; before, I didn't know it. That's the difference. I'm not sure if it was the atmosphere there, or the direction, or our ages, but we'd become actors.
>
> "Some of the films were overproduced, especially the junior Busby Berkeley dance things. Also, it seemed like there were so many more executives around telling everybody what to do."[2]

Unfortunately, while the series was still a wonderfully profitable and popular entertainment in America, MGM was treating it as yet another cog in its corporate machinery. People were assigned to it, but it was never anybody's baby as it had been for Hal Roach. He later admitted, " 'They had thousands of people at Metro, but they didn't have anybody down there to supervise the films and take any interest in their production in the same way I had.' "[3]

The second reality was that, for whatever reason, the screenplays arriving in our in-boxes just were not as good. Stories began to be contrived, too adult and artificial. Most crippling, by later accounts, was a growing trend toward preachy or "message" scripts. America was slowly drifting toward involvement in World War II, and *Our Gang* shorts began to subliminally tell audiences to support the war effort. *Doin' Their Bit,* released in 1942, blatantly shilled for the USO (United Service Organizations) and was a flag-waving exercise in jingoism. A year earlier, the *Gang* was straitjacketed into an irritating little short called *1-2-3 Go!* that was little more than a school safety educational film. *Time Out for Lessons* has a chastised Alfalfa not getting to play football because he earned bad grades. (No surprise there.) Looking almost directly into the camera, he moralizes to his pals: "Listen, gang, from now on we take time out for lessons!" "Ten-minute morality plays," one reviewer grumpily dubbed them. In his astute, full-length analysis, Leonard Maltin additionally concluded, "Every time an *Our Gang* plot is pegged to the idea of 'teaching the kids a lesson,' the results are below par."[4]

According to Tommy Bond, once the franchise dropped its perennial good guy versus bad guy theme, the series was doomed. Of course, for Butch, being the villain was very lucrative, so I'm not surprised he would come to that conclusion! The concept of two gents vying for one lady dated clear back to a 1930 story entitled *The First Seven Years,* where Jackie Cooper found himself competing with rival Donald "Speck" Haines for the affections of cherubic Mary Ann Jackson. Of course, Alfalfa, Butch, and I raised the Olympics of Love to an art form, and now that spark seemed to be missing.

With all this in mind, *Our Gang* parents and fans were pleased when a nice little gem entitled *Duel Personalities* began to be filmed right around the same time the studio was shooting *Gone With the Wind.* Playing off the hypnotism craze that was currently hot around

America, the idea was to have a famous practitioner of the art work his mental craft on Alfalfa. Soon the dreamy-eyed youngster is convinced that he is actually the swashbuckling d'Artagnan and one of the legendary musketeers. (Errol Flynn's *The Adventures of Robin Hood* had just hit theaters the year before.)

Immediately this gives Alfalfa the courage to challenge Butch to a duel to redress the outrage that his enemy has—yet again—tried to steal Darla from him. (When a running gag worked for us, we generally stayed with it for a long time!) With his patented lip curl, Butch accepts the challenge, and both boys begin sharpening their swords.

Darla, whose character has grown increasingly fickle over the years, is giddy with the romantic idea that two boys are soon going to be parrying and thrusting over *her*! Her excitement ebbs, though, when a friend points out that one of her suitors might actually end up stone-cold dead, blood oozing from a fatal wound. *Oh.* She hadn't thought of that.

Repentant, she rushes over to the clubhouse, ready to cancel the love match title, when she overhears the boys scheming. Apparently Professor Delmore's hypnotic spell is beginning to wear off, and Alfalfa and Butch have agreed that no dame is worth risking their red American blood over. Their alternative scheme is to duel with guns— actually harmless cap pistols—and simultaneously fall to the ground, feigning mortal wounds. Whichever boy Darla rushes to rescue, they decide, will be the victor and will get to take her to the show.

Once again, I see my two favorite script words: *Enter Waldo.* George Sidney counted me down. *Three, two, one, go!*—and I walked into the story right at the close. Playing along with the tense showdown, Darla witnesses the faux carnage and then turns on her heel. "Come on, Waldo," she flirts. "*You* take me to the show instead." As the two of us walk away arm in arm, she calls out over her shoulder, "Don't forget to bury them." It was a cute episode, and for the third time, I proudly notched a mental DH in my actor's belt.

Romantic victor or no, it was a true delight for me to work with Darla in Our Gang. She went on to craft a fine career from her singing voice, appearing on Broadway, various radio shows, and in nightclub performances. She had an amazing three-octave vocal range, and supplemented her income by doing voice-overs and TV commercials. If you remember the Chicken of the Sea mermaid jingle, well, that was our Darla. I was as crushed as her myriad of fans when I heard she had passed away from a bout of hepatitis at the early age of forty-seven.

Dual Personalities was a rare MGM success because it returned to the successful timeliness that had sparked earlier triumphs for the franchise. Very early on, the seventh film in the series, The Big Show, had our pint-sized pros successfully imitating Charlie Chaplin, who had been a phenomenon in 1923. That same year, Lodge Night was astute enough to quietly ridicule the Ku Klux Klan with its fraternal order, the Cluck Cluck Klams. When the Great Depression hit the country in late 1929, the next show Our Gang trotted out was entitled Moan & Groan, Inc.

We barely caught our breath before Jack Chertok, our new MGM producer, had another film assignment for us. I was written into Cousin Wilbur but didn't really have much to do except sit around and be part of the scenery for returning hero Scotty Beckett. Almost exactly the same age as I was, he had joined Our Gang in 1934 and was heralded as one of the cutest kids to ever play in the troupe. (A distinction that was never assigned to me, that's for sure.) For some reason, he had drifted out of the show in 1936 and now was suddenly walking through the MGM portals for the first time.

The story has Scotty playing Alfalfa's prissy cousin, "Wilbur," in a confrontation between the Gang and its perennial antagonists, Butch and Woim. The refined Wilbur asks why the All 4 One Club currently has only four members, then he suggests that President Spanky needs to provide more club benefits. He comes up with the idea of offering a kind of injury insurance to all the kids, which will make them rich in case of a black eye or busted nose. But the two intruding hooligans plot to wound and maim every single kid in the neighborhood and thereby break the club's insurance bank.

Again, I had little to do in this story, but reviewers did observe later that Scotty's essential challenge was to "be a Waldo"—a task he achieved admirably. My slender connection with him and ZaSu Pitts got me a shred of celluloid screen time later that year in a film they did entitled *Mickey, the Kid*. It saddened Scotty's many admirers around the world to later read how he spiraled into a life of drug abuse, multiple marriages, and brutal divorces. In 1968, he was beaten by an assailant and checked into a hospital; he died at the age of thirty-eight.

Even as youngsters in our make-believe cocoon, we heard similar tales, and they made me think again about my own life and the fragility of my spiritual existence in the world of movies. Horror tales about drunken brawls and drugs occasionally seeped onto the *Our Gang* set as an alumnus would hit the skids. Stymie, so beloved a part of the Roach empire, had drifted into a hardscrabble existence of high school drugs and gangs; he later became addicted to heroin and spent time in prison before finally getting clean and rehabilitating his life.

I didn't know it at the time, but a newcomer to the *Our Gang* world was going to epitomize all the scars that Hollywood was capable of inflicting. Right after *Cousin Wilbur,* Robert Blake, a five-year-old they dubbed "Mickey Gubitosi" was dropped into our current story, a Boy Scouts type of adventure redubbed *Joy Scouts.* He was a sad-faced kid whose chief screen characteristic seemed to be that of a whiner. He had bumped around as an extra on this film project and that, but finally lucked out one day on *Our Gang* when another actor simply couldn't get his line of dialogue to come out right. Apparently, Mickey's folks agreed with my own dad in adopting the credo "Don't be shy!" When the nameless kid kept flubbing, Mickey blurted out, "I can say that!"

Shrugging, the director tossed the first kid, stuttering his protests, to the sidelines and gave Mickey the part. From then on, he was a regular, taking over for the retiring Porky. I enjoyed acting with him in my final five films for *Our Gang*. As the franchise wound down to its conclusion in 1944, Mickey ended up being the series leader. He was one of the few who went on to have hugely successful adult careers: he had a good part in Humphrey Bogart's *The Treasure of the Sierra Madre*, nabbed the title role of Perry Smith in the adaptation of Truman Capote's *In Cold Blood*, and then won an Emmy playing *Baretta* on ABC for four television seasons with his trademark cockatoo perched on his shoulder.

Robert Blake's adult success is somewhat ironic because reviewers generally panned his performance as Mickey in our MGM shows. He was a sour little kid, whose phony cry-on-demand screen moments were hard to watch. Leonard Maltin, who had occasion to review the entire body of his work as both a child and adult, cryptically observed, "Although he emerged as a fine actor in the 1960s and 1970s, his histrionics in *Our Gang*—'whiny and obnoxious'—were soon to play a part in the series' demise."[5]

In his personal life, Blake tumbled into a private hell, running away from home at the age of fourteen and falling prey to both drug abuse and alcoholism. He told talk show host Merv Griffin that he had snorted dope, sold it, everything. He finally ended up arrested in 2002 on a charge of murdering his wife, Bonnie Lee Bakley. (He was acquitted three years later after an extended celebrity trial but was subsequently convicted in a civil case, where the burden of proof was not as high.)

There were other seamy stories about the high price exacted by cinema fame. Gus Meins, one of our directors, left the studio in a rage over some policy dispute with Mr. Roach, and later committed suicide, shocking all of us.

A really nice lady, Peggy Shannon, dropped by the MGM lot to do a bit part as Mickey's mom for a story called *All About Hash*. Within a year, she was dead of acute alcoholism; when her husband came home and discovered her with an empty glass in her dead hand, he, too, took his own life. So these were sober reminders to me that I was living in a dangerous career bubble where godlessness and fast living were the casually accepted norms. I was trying to hang on to some of my new ideas and a very fragile Christian faith with some help from Carmelo and my pals at church.

Chapter Eleven

DOUBLE TAKES

The air was crisp and cold in Griffith Park as Dad bent over his portable stove. I was famished and waited impatiently as he poured pancake batter onto the bubbling griddle.

It was a regular Sunday morning routine for the two of us. Mom was a late riser, and on weekends, she hardly ever made an appearance before eleven. She had surprised us both with the announcement that she was pregnant, so we were glad to let her luxuriate in bed and pamper herself. Dad and I would enjoy a few hours on our own. Pancakes in the park was our favorite routine, and we always liked hiking clear up to the top of the hill, where the new Griffith Observatory had been constructed just five years earlier. I never tired of watching the Foucault pendulum as it slowly swung back and forth, knocking over pegs as it imperceptibly shifted according to the rotation of the earth.

This particular weekend I was getting ready for what I was now sensing might be one of my few final scripts for *Our Gang*. Jack Chertok, our producer, had already called to let Alfalfa's folks and mine know that—nothing personal—the end was probably near. They might hang on to Spanky for a few more episodes simply because too much cast change might be wrenching, but with so many of us now ten years old or more, pink slips were inexorably heading toward our mailboxes.

I thought about my buddy Porky, who had "retired" after *Auto Antics* about a year earlier. It had been a wrenching time for his family, and even as an innocent kid, he knew what it felt like to be abruptly dropped. " 'It's rough,' " he later confided to a friend. " 'The M-G-M limousine stops coming to your house . . . and you wonder why the world has ceased loving you so suddenly at age seven!' "[1] As a first-grader, toting a lunch bucket to school, he was already carrying around unemployment check stubs.

Dad and I talked about it as we drenched our pancakes in gooey syrup and half-frozen little chunks of butter. There were just a few scattered picnickers here and there this early on a Sunday, and Dad was philosophical about my future.

"Don't worry, doll," he said easily between bites. "You've had a good run. I mean, I think you were in some great films, you and Spanky and the guys." He sipped from his glass of orange juice. "You'll get other work."

I nodded. It was nice working on a series for which you had one assigned character role and a lot of friends. Freelancing in Hollywood was a lot tougher; months might go by with no work at all. It took hustle, a lot of apple-polishing, and an aggressive agent manning the phones. I would have to adjust to the public school system after years of being pampered by Mrs. Carter. And, of course, the Smith family had enjoyed it tremendously as Hal Roach's weekly paychecks steadily climbed from fifty dollars to seventy-five dollars. I knew Mom and Dad hadn't tucked away very much of that cinema loot—we lived very comfortably there in 1940—and it would be hard to suddenly have that cash flow dry up.

"We'll worry about that if and when it happens," Dad assured me, opening a plastic container filled with Mom's special strawberry topping. "Come on, kid, let's finish up with some of this sugar goo." He grinned at me. "Then I'll race you up the hill."

I hadn't been Waldo for a few months now, so in March I was thankful to get to reprise my role. Strangely, the writers had earlier come up with a story entitled *Alfalfa's Double,* in which trick photography let Alfalfa play two parts at once. Cornelius, a visiting millionaire kid who looks exactly like our cowlicked friend, is a new arrival in town. In a spin-off of the timeless *The Prince and the Pauper* theme, Alfalfa and "Alfalfa II" decide to switch roles and sample life from the other side of the tracks. The basic idea is that Alfalfa has to now play me! "Our resemblance is rather striking," the visiting Cornelius observes. Alfalfa states, "Yeah, and we look alike too." I must say that Alfalfa handled himself well in a Waldo-type role, but I was now ready to reclaim my glasses and book of poetry.

The Big Premiere, directed by Edward Cahn, has me, the rich kid who owns a movie camera, trying to shoot a *Our Gang* movie after we're all shooed away and disinvited from a big Hollywood gala event. So, as our troupe is wont to do, we create our own! I'm busily cranking our way through the *Our Gang* version of *The Mysteeryus Mistry.* We have our own stars and starlets, our searchlights and red carpet, and even our own wet-cement sidewalk for celebrities to endorse with their handprints. Naturally, megastar Buckwheat gets stuck in it when he tries to embed his footprints there for posterity.

Unfortunately, as the madcap adventure unfolds, Waldo runs out of film halfway through the story. There are plenty of gags sprinkled throughout, the best of which is a comic actress, Ethelreda Leopold, getting her sequined gown splattered with the cementlike goo when a cop chase skids its way through our own Walk of Fame.

By most accounts, it was a rather thin story, but *Our Gang* directors had long ago learned how to make a lot out of a little. One stan-

Let's put on a show! The Big Premiere *was one of my last* Our Gang *films for MGM. My job is going to be to run the movie camera—except I have no film. I'm just to Buckwheat's left with a glassy look on my face.*

dard gimmick to stretch out a joke was to simply show a second actor's facial response to the original gag. Someone falls in a vat of cement—that's funny! Alfalfa gives a goggle-eyed look—and that's funny a second time. Two laughs for the price of one. In *Our Gang* movie parlance, these facial double takes were dubbed "takems." The scripts soon began to use that term almost as official direction, with writers hitching a "takem" onto the original gag. Almost everyone on the set agreed that Buckwheat was truly the king of "takems." If they wanted a *really* outlandish response, they would drop the directions *taking it big* into the screenplay.

Maltin's meticulous research on the intricacies of *Our Gang* scripting soon deciphered the code. "*Our Gang* scripts . . . [had] a liberal sprinkling of slapstick jargon," he writes, "indigenous to the colorful comedy heritage on the Hal Roach lot. . . . It's rare when a page from a Roach script won't employ terms like the '108' (a staggering pratfall), the 'burn' (an angry reaction), the 'slow burn' . . . the 'takem' (a pronounced facial reaction—Spanky and Buckwheat execute it often in *Two Too Young*), and the 'double takem,' or 'taking it big' (slight initial reaction, hesitation, then full, wide-eyed comprehension that builds)."[2] Spanky even had a patented little head bob that preceded his owl-eyed "takems" whenever our makeshift hotrods ran off the road or someone's pants fell down around their ankles.

Besides the steroid effect we tried to get by juicing up our laughs this way, Alfalfa had his own patented facial tics that he employed whenever the story called for him to be around Darla. Being Waldo, my own inscrutable demeanor never seemed to vary much, pretty girls or no. Whenever I won Miss Hood's heart, it was because of my bookish charm, not my grimaces and blushing swoons. But Maltin describes with relish how Alfalfa had an entire catalog of mannerisms that colored his moments of romantic prowess. "An Alfalfa 'fig bar,' " he explains, "calls for an exaggerated coyness and a series of embarrassment pauses at talking with some charmer, usually Darla Hood, and especially while being paid a compliment, whether deserved or no."[3]

He was in full "fig bar" mode during *Hearts Are Thumps*, when he had to reluctantly choke down Darla's soap sandwich. It was observed that a good thirty years later a second country bumpkin named Jim Nabors shamelessly borrowed Alfalfa's "fig bar" shy shtick whenever his Gomer Pyle character was around the off-key but beautiful Lou-Ann Poovie. Do you remember his drawn-out *Gawwww-lee*? Pure Alfalfa.[4]

I spent most of that summer away from the MGM lot and enjoying the long lazy days that mark the wonder of Southern California.

There was a gathering military storm across the Atlantic, with Hitler pushing his way toward England, but I was blissfully unaware. I read a lot of adventure stories and an occasional Adventist kid magazine forwarded on to me by Grandpa, and I got my parents to take me to the beach as often as possible. Mom would sit in a lounge chair guarding my baby brother, Dennis, as Dad and I tossed a baseball back and forth and built sand castles. He would grill smoke-flavored hot dogs that were zestfully crunchy, and we would contentedly chew our way through them as the sun slowly set over the ocean. On the way back to the car, I'd occasionally notice an unusual rock, which I'd tote back home and add to my collection.

I was just a fair athlete, and my work in movies made it impossible to really try anything like Little League baseball. But I listened to games on a big radio we kept out on the back porch. I loved going into our backyard and fantasizing about being in the big leagues. We had a long brick wall bordering our property, and in my mind's eye I had marked out four large bricks that I figured were a reasonable strike zone.

Peering grimly into that tiny bit of space, I imagined I was on the mound for the World Series. With my flair for imagination, I would do a CBS play-by-play as I hurled nasty sliders at the bricks.

"DiMaggio at the plate, count's even at one and one." I would kick at an imaginary clod of Yankee dust. "He seems to have no answer today for Smith's curve. Into the windup, here's the one-one, and it's a strike! Joe just looked at the ball as if to say, 'I can't hit what I can't see.' Will Smith come back with another curve, or will he blow Joltin' Joe away with his legendary fastball?" That kind of thing. Even if my wobbling fastballs missed the designated bricks, I would often give myself a strikeout anyway if the situation was crucial enough; that's the benefit of being your own umpire. I remember pitching my way through titanic baseball struggles between America and the Soviet

Union—and somehow the United States always won.

From the earliest days, Mom had insisted that I take piano lessons, and I endured a weekly session with Mr. Samuel Ball, a well-trained classical musician. He tutored me in the classics, such as "To a Wild Rose" by MacDowell and "Serenade," composed by Moszkowski. I had to practice two hours each day, and I sometimes put in a bit of extra time even beyond that, so that I'd be free to attend Saturday matinees.

Carmelo's mom kept driving us to church most weekends, and I found myself often pondering the ideas in the pastor's sermons. I was intrigued by the idea of heaven and all that it seemed to promise. Mom and Dad seldom referred to it or to the idea that a faithful believer could live forever. Sitting around the dinner table, Dad would occasionally ruminate about the "Man upstairs"; his entire theology about eternal life didn't go beyond Saint Peter jokes he'd heard at the office. Yet both Mom and Dad seemed entirely willing for me to dress up each Sunday and leave them to the thick weekend edition of the *Los Angeles Times*.

I made a perfunctory appearance in *The New Pupil*, a smallish bit of fluff, written mostly for Alfalfa's benefit. He and Spanky both chase after this new girl who comes to school, and it's a four-way traffic jam of confused puppy love with Sally and Darla fending off both boys' advances. Our visiting beauty queen was a nine-year-old cutie named Juanita Quigley, whose nickname around town was "Baby Jane." She hung around Hollywood for several years after her brief stint with us and reached her career pinnacle when landing a teen part in *National Velvet*, playing the sister of both Elizabeth Taylor and Angela Lansbury. In a foreshadowing of my own spiritual quest, Juanita later ditched her contract with Universal Studios and became a Roman Catholic nun—Sister Quentin Rita!

Chapter Twelve

EARLY RETIREMENT

"All of us are really going to miss you, Waldo."

It was Hal Roach himself, who had driven over to the MGM studio lot as we were wrapping up my final film. Even though he no longer had any legal connection to the long-running franchise, it was still Mr. Roach who had created the Waldo character in his mind and who had chosen me to play the part. Now that it was over, I thought it was incredibly gracious on his part to stop by and wish me well.

During my all-too-brief time of actually being his employee, Mr. Roach had diligently looked after each of us. Years later, Darla described how our lovable boss pampered the stars in his acting troupe; at Christmastime, each of us could basically state our dream—and he would bulldoze the fabled Hollywood sign if necessary to get it done. She had once shyly asked for a dollhouse; somehow his wires got crossed, and on December 25, he presented her with a full-size children's playhouse. The prop department had constructed a huge ten-by-twelve-foot kiddie mansion for her, and it took a moving van to transport it to the Hood residence. So it was no surprise to me that Hal Roach had made time out of his schedule to come and say Good-bye to me. After one more short, Alfalfa was slated to say *Adios* from

I exit Our Gang on a sour note. Waldo's Last Stand is a real clinker. Robert Blake, little "Mickey," standing between Darla and Buckwheat, survived his own petulant acting in Our Gang and had a big Hollywood career as Baretta.

Our Gang as well; his farewell performance was just six weeks later in *Kiddie Kure.*

The studio had sprung for a huge chocolate cake and several tubs of ice cream. Several of the parents were milling around, and my folks chatted with them about the future of their Darwood Kaye.

I had mixed feelings as I shook hands with one after another of the various stars who had played a role in *Waldo's Last Stand.* Yes, that was actually the title of my final episode. Hal Law had written a one-reel story in which Waldo is trying to raise money by operating a lemonade stand. This was actually a four-year-old retread of an idea Mr. Roach had filmed earlier entitled *The Lucky Corner.* Unfortunately,

I was going out of the *Gang* universe with somewhat of a clinker as the last item in my résumé; by all reviews, the 1936 short was a much better comedy than mine. The earlier film employed yet another of Hollywood's favorite gag gimmicks: the "spit-take" in which a perfectly timed surprise causes an actor to spray out whatever he's just been drinking. (This isn't really apple juice? *Splat!* Who's pregnant? *Splat!* That kind of thing.)

My final show has me looking more down-to-earth in a simple striped T-shirt—I still did wear horn-rimmed glasses though—and trying to get my own franchise on solid financial footing. Unfortunately, the lemonade business has turned sour on me; Waldo has no customers. But that's the beauty of being in *Our Gang;* they can fix anything.

Spanky returns us to the age-old solution: "Let's put on a show!" All that applause should build up a powerful thirst in our theater patrons and send them rushing to the concession stand. Darla offers to sing, we bring in a barbershop quartet called the Singing Waiters, and there are various other song-and-dance features. There's just one problem: we hire so many vaudevillian pros that there's no one left to be in the audience!

Actually, Waldo's last stand does have a shot at one customer; his name is Froggy. Billy Laughlin had just joined the cast two episodes earlier and was to stay by until the end of the franchise. His signature claim to fame was a prematurely gravelly voice, made that way, some suggested, by a faulty tonsillectomy. Hence the nickname Froggy. He had crossed eyes, which forced him to wear coke-bottle glasses— yet somehow, he had parlayed those two handicaps into a lucrative movie career. It was a shocker to hear, just eight years later, that he'd been killed when a truck hit him while he riding a motor scooter in La Puente.

As *Waldo*'s great extravaganza is going on, all for the purpose of creating thirst in this one raspy-voiced kid, Froggy just won't give in.

After the Our Gang *franchise released me, I got tiny parts in pictures here and there. The pay was good, but the roles were microscopic. I'm in a picture entitled* Victory *with actor-director John Cromwell.*

Nothing works. His sales resistance is fireproof. Spanky virtually force-feeds him some salted crackers; the gang stokes up a floor heater that's been secreted under his chair. Alfalfa even tries his hand at subliminal influence, crooning his unsubtle way through "How Dry I Am" and "Drink to Me Only With Thine Eyes." But no sale. Over and over, Froggy repeats, "I don't have no money, and besides, it's too hot in here."

It would have been a great comedy to end on, except for one hard fact: it wasn't funny. Reviewers mostly forgave me for my part in it, since Waldo wasn't a truly comic role anyway. But it was difficult to salvage a script in which the key punch line has Spanky looking around in despair and observing, "Nobody came to our show 'cause everybody in the neighborhood is *in* the show!"

Our director, Edward Cahn, did all the usual things to help save a weak story line. One sure way to save a mediocre plot was to ramp

I laugh on cue with my fellow child actors.

up the cute animal quotient. Many an *Our Gang* short had been re-
vived by the screen talents of our own Pete the Pup. Directors quickly
figured out that a sagging moment could be followed by a quick cut
to Pete, who seemed to have perfected his own canine "takem."
Other times, stories that didn't have quite enough of a plot to get to
the requisite ten minute could be padded by just showing a new cute
star frolicking with any animal for whatever amount of screen time
needed to be soaked up.

I already mentioned that Pete the Pup enjoyed a salary most of us
would have eaten a plate of dog food to get our hands on. Stymie had
his derby, Alfalfa his cowlick, I had those fancy glasses, and Pete always
had a lopsided circle around one eye. Truth be told, there were at least
three Petes through the years, and the circle was fake. Let me explain.
The bulldog Mr. Roach originally hired came from a previous film series

entitled *Buster Brown,* and the circle had been painted on with permanent dye. Roach actually didn't like the ring, but it was a permanent fixture, so it stayed. When other dogs were later hired to reprise the role, a new matching ring always had to be applied before shooting. In one film, some flubbed shots had to be redone later—what we grumblingly called "insert shots." An inexperienced makeup lady inadvertently put the ring on the wrong eye! When Roach spotted the mistake, he told our film lab they had to flip that entire scene so that the story would look consistent.

Interestingly, someone unearthed a tattered photo of a delighted fourteen-year-old fan posing with Pete the Pup; it turned out to be a youthful Fred Rogers, who later had all sorts of pets visit his *Neighborhood.*

In any case, I blush to confess that my final film was spotty enough in its comedic punch that we needed almost an entire Noah's ark to come rescue the laugh track. Right at the end a mule brays, and the kids all burst into prompted laughter.

Ouch. Yes, I'll have another piece of cake, Mr. Cahn. What a note to end on.

Still, it all paid the same. Studio records indicated later that *Waldo's Last Stand* cost $21,438 to make and turned a profit of just over $12,000. A little bit of that was mine! My parents drove me home with a final check from MGM sitting on the dashboard of the car. Mom had the baby in her arms and put her head on Dad's shoulder as we glided our way out of a most pleasant era of life.

Where would events take me next? Was God going to abruptly show His cards and give me a new role?

Fortunately, one slender bit of feature film acting had already been dangled in front of me. A studio company called Republic Pictures was assembling a cast to do a musical story called *Barnyard Follies* as a star vehicle for their own version of Shirley Temple, a teenager

I didn't care for the name Darwood, but it beat the character name of Stinky, which I endured in a lame film entitled G-Men. *I've still got those glasses.*

named Mary Lee. The film was one long infomercial for the 4-H Club, but the good news was that the producer wanted to borrow Alfalfa to play himself in a couple of scenes. As luck would have it, they had room for me as well, basically just as an extra, and my on-the-ball agent, Mr. Sherril, quickly brought a contract over for us to sign. The entire thing took only a few days of shooting time, but the pay was good, and it eased my adjustment into regular life. I also grabbed an envelope filled with cash for a short piece of filming with John Cromwell, who had just finished directing *Abe Lincoln in Illinois*. He was heading up a dark drama, *Victory*, based on a Joseph Conrad novel about a recluse on a Dutch East Indies island, and my parents proudly displayed a studio glossy, showing me wearing a tuxedo and standing next to the actor-director.

In the meantime, my baby brother was already helping to make a

Still "Stinky."

living! Ever the alert entrepreneur, Dad had pulled a few strings, and Mr. Sherril had landed Dennis a bit part—as a cooing infant, of course—in a 1940 Henry Fonda story entitled *Lillian Russell*. I couldn't help but wonder if this was how the torch was supposed to be passed.

I had already transferred to public school, so fall of 1940 had me making the adjustment to regular classroom life. I endured the expected teasing as classmates tried to get away with calling me Waldo or Dagwood, but my teachers stoutly insisted that the kids refer to me as Kenny. Even though I hadn't legally changed my name, I had decided a year earlier that the "Kaye" I used in Hollywood might as well become a name I actually liked. So my new friends in sixth grade began calling me Kenny, and after a few resistant occasions at home, Mom and Dad followed suit. I got into junior varsity sports, and I

I got little bits in several features for Republic Pictures. Here my glasses and I get paid for being in Barnyard Follies. Even my own parents didn't attend some of those turkeys.

liked playing with the baby on Sunday afternoons after church.

I was shaking Christmas packages under the tree one evening that December when the phone rang. I could tell from the one-way conversation that Mom was talking with her father back east, and I surmised from her reactions that there was a foot of Nebraska snow on Grandpa's front porch. After a few minutes of chatting, she held the phone out for me. "Want to say Hi to your grandpa?"

Trading the baby for the phone receiver, I eagerly blurted out a Hello.

"How you doin', Kenny?"

"I'm fine." Back in 1940, long distance connections were a little crackly; it sounded like there must be icicles dangling from the telephone lines. "I'm just playing with Dennis."

"He's a cutie all right," Grandpa praised. "Your mom sent us some pictures, and Grandma has them all over the piano." He laughed. "Some of you too."

He asked me about school and how I was doing being in a regular classroom where "normal" kids had to attend. "Did the principal roll out some red carpeting for you the first day?" he teased. I always thought he had a really nice sense of humor, especially for a preacher.

"Yes, I'm still going," I responded when he asked me about church. "Well, most of the time. Last weekend Mom and I went to the Santa Monica Pier instead." I blushed a bit but knew he wouldn't bawl me out. "She let me ride the merry-go-round three times." Even as I said it, I felt kind of silly; should a ten-year-old still like going round and round on a carousel with mechanical horsies?

Grandpa laughed, but I sensed that he was about to give me a gentle *zinger*. "Well, you know, honey, I just always find that if we put God's business first, and merry-go-rounds second, that's a pretty good lineup. I'll bet Mom would take you over to the pier any other time they were open. I imagine those folks at the church just don't know what to do with themselves when Mr. Ken Smith is away."

"Yeah." I liked how Grandpa knew how to give me a boost toward the things of God without sounding like he was mad. "There's a big Christmas program at church this weekend, and Carmelo's mom is taking us. I think a missionary band from Brazil is playing some carols."

"That sounds terrific." Grandpa's voice faded for a moment as the holiday phone lines trembled with all the traffic. "Are you still practicing your piano?"

"Uh-huh."

We chatted just a moment longer; I knew that long-distance telephone rates were painfully expensive and that a preacher couldn't afford to just sit around gabbing between Nebraska and Los Angeles. He wrapped up the visit, as he always did, by telling me he was praying for Dennis and me. "You guys are just the specialest things in the world to your old grandma and me," he admitted. "And you know, Ken, I sometimes go for long walks in the snow and just think about the amazing thing God is going to do with your life."

I waited, not knowing what to say in response.

"There's a reason why the Lord chose to put so many overflowing talents into one kid," he went on. "I just know it; there's a reason. And the reason wasn't so that you could just walk around taking insults from this Alfalfa character. You know? There's something else there, Kenny—and I believe in my heart that in the next few years, you're going to one day look in front of you, and you'll see a new kind of road. And Jesus will be saying, 'Come along with Me.' "

"Uh-huh." The twinkling lights of the tree were reflecting against our living room window, but my mind was transfixed by my grandfather's challenge to me. *A road before me?* Even though I was just ten, I did feel something calling to me. I'd spent three years helping Spanky glue fat ladies' skirts to their chairs and making children laugh. *Is an All-knowing God up in heaven actually aware of my Hollywood résumé, my growing portfolio down at the Mitchell Gertz Agency? Will God approvingly stand by as I segue now into hardened adult films, with their sordid stories of salacious deals and romantic betrayal? Or is He going to abduct me from my film career and force me to become a preacher or something?*

My heart was all mixed-up as we said Goodbye. My tender life, seasoned by a bare decade, already faced the crossroads of losing the *Our Gang* connection and having to graduate to Hollywood's big time. Now Grandpa, with all the good wishes in the world and with a Bible in his lap, seemed to be telling me that God might be inexorably pulling me toward a second critical moment-of-life decision.

It felt like a lot for a kid my age to handle, and I went back to the Christmas tree and tried to figure out what that really long package with my name on it could possibly have inside. I was relieved that it was the wrong shape for a choir robe.

Chapter Thirteen

I Loved Lucy

The months of 1941 slipped easily past me, as I adjusted to life without *Our Gang*. Mom and Dad didn't take us out to eat as often as before, but except for that, I really didn't sense any financial void from not having piles of MGM money lying around the house. I had always been an apt student, and homework very seldom cut into my evenings at home with Dennis. I joined the school's fledgling tap dancing troupe, and we did a couple of shows for parents and community friends. Just before school let out in June, Miss Beacham arranged for us to do a performance at a retirement center in Temple City, and the old folks gushed over us until I almost needed some fresh air.

One old man with high-water pants pointed a bony finger in my face. "I know you," he said with a deliberate twinkle. "You and those boys. In the movies."

"Really?"

"Oh yes." His gnarly hands trembled as he placed them on my shoulders. "You were the nice one. With the glasses, no? You kept that fat boy out of trouble."

"Uh-huh." I grinned. "That was me."

"What was your name, boy?" His patchy mustache wiggled as he tried to pull back a fading memory. "Wally, wasn't it?"

"No, Waldo."

"Yes! Yes! You were that Waldo boy. You were the best one."

I had to admit that I enjoyed such moments. The staff bombarded us with glazed doughnuts and a watery berry punch before waving goodbye. My pals and I belted out "You Are My Sunshine," which was a big Wayne King hit on the radio that summer, as the school bus threaded its way through Los Angeles traffic and back to the campus.

After many months of cinematic inactivity, it was a relief that July when Mr. Sherril finally called with a job offer. Again, it was the tiniest part imaginable, but he had heard through the buzzing Hollywood grapevine that Twentieth Century Fox was getting ready to roll cameras on *Remember the Day,* a patriotic film that had been quickly put together for one of Tinseltown's hottest starlets, Claudette Colbert. It was a love story with political overtones, and had Colbert acting the role of a schoolteacher who goes to Washington to visit a presidential candidate who had been in her eighth-grade class long before.

I spent a few pleasant days on the lot of Fox, playing the part of a student in a few of Colbert's flashback scenes and shamelessly ogling the very appealing lead actress. She was winsomely beautiful, a French-born performer who had worked hard to overcome a slight lisp. Six years before we met on the set, she had taken home a coveted Best Actress in a Leading Role Oscar statuette for her performance in *It Happened One Night.* I hadn't seen the movie, but I heard some of the stagehands gossiping about the famous scene in which she and Clark Gable had been stranded in the countryside. "I'll show you how to hitch a ride," she had boasted; and tugging up her skirt to show off a bit of leg, the couple very quickly was picked up and driven back into town. By now she was the most established star in town; she had rejected a multiyear deal that offered two hundred thousand

Finally—my one good role! I'm Killer, a military cadet and resident nerd in Best Foot Forward.

dollars a year, figuring correctly that she could earn almost that much per picture. The other extras and I joked about just following her over to the commissary, hoping that twenty-dollar bills would fall out of her pocket.

The film opened on Christmas Day, just two and a half weeks after the horrific bombing of Pearl Harbor, so the title, *Remember the Day*, had a cruel irony to it. I remember sitting with my parents listening to President Roosevelt telling a stunned nation that the seventh of that month was a day that would live in infamy. I couldn't help but wonder if World War II was going to drag on so long that my school friends and I might all be shipped overseas to fight against the vast Japanese army or Hitler's *Luftwaffe*.

Only a few weeks later, personal tragedy struck. A telegram arrived one evening informing us that Grandma Kite had just passed away. Mom thought she should travel to Nebraska for the funeral, but Grandpa said that he would rather just have Grandma's funeral and burial and then come out and be with us for a little while.

We didn't have a large house, certainly not by Hollywood standards, but I willingly moved in with my little brother so that Grandpa could have my bedroom. He stayed until almost March and helped Mom by playing with Dennis and doing some of the light chores. He would take both of us to the park and hand us dimes to ride the little mechanical horse by Sinclair Market.

Whenever we sat down to supper, Mom would say, "Dad?" We would all hold hands, and he would say a short prayer of thanks for the meal. I know he wished he could gather the family for worship each night, but he diplomatically held back. Sometimes when I passed by my bedroom, I would see him in there praying by himself or simply reading in the New Testament, making some notes in a small pad he kept by the bed.

Three weekends in a row, Mom let him borrow the family car, and he drove us boys over to an Adventist church in Van Nuys. The preacher was a wonderful people person, and he made a big fuss over Dennis and me. The youth group was planning a big progressive party, where all the kids went from one home to another, playing various games and sampling different food at each one. Grandpa dutifully drove me all around town, and it was nearly midnight before we got home. I was intrigued by this seemingly parallel world, where people spoke so easily about their heavenly hopes.

Grandpa gave all of us big hugs as we saw him off on his train heading back east. "This was fun, Kenny," he managed, his voice husky as he told me Goodbye. "You helped your old grandpa get through a pretty rough patch." His right hand clutched my shoulder. "But you know, Jesus is going to make sure we get together with Grandma again. Won't be long now."

"I know." All of his talk about heaven and resurrection was very new to me, but he spoke of these things as if they were settled fact. We waved until his train slid out of sight.

Nothing else came along for my sputtering film career until after I had graduated from eighth grade. My agent popped by one Friday afternoon and offered to take all four of us out to lunch. Dennis was toddling around pretty well by then, and the waitress at the Italian restaurant brought a booster chair for him.

Over plates of steaming pasta, Mr. Sherril told how MGM had its eye on a hot Broadway play called *Best Foot Forward*. "I guess they been doing boffo business in New York," he told us as we twirled strands of spaghetti onto our forks. "It's a musical farce. I haven't seen it, but my cousin has—and the songs are just great. It ran, sold out, for about a year."

"Who's in it?" Dad was astute at following the trade journals and knew most of the famous actors on both coasts.

"Well, June Allyson's the big Broadway name, and she's already agreed to come out here and be in the movie as well," the agent confirmed. "But we're lucky, 'cause the whole thing was originally going to land in Columbia's lap." We all knew they were the other major studio in town.

Lew consulted some notes he had on a yellow pad. Phone numbers were scrawled all over it; he was an indefatigable deal maker for his various clients around town. "From what my guys are telling me, Harry Cohn had planned to buy the rights to the show and then stick Rita Hayworth in it."

Mom brightened; Rita Hayworth was one of her favorite stars. "Oh, I love her!"

"Yeah, she's good," the older man nodded. "For some reason that all fell through. I mean, they had the Glenn Miller Orchestra all lined up to play, plus Shirley Temple was going to costar. But somehow, *kerflooey*."

It's not my tuba playing that made Best Foot Forward *a successful musical. The hot jazz of Harry James's band and Lucille Ball's star appeal carried the day.*

We all knew that sometimes it happened that way. Blockbuster deals could very slowly move their way through from backroom dealing to storyboarding to hiring to—nothing. One false move or some payback for some rivalry gone sour could shred months and even years of painstaking planning. A hundred lunches like the one we were having could go up in a cloud of smoke.

Dad poured himself another drink of soda from the pitcher set in the center of the table. "So how do we come in?"

Lew grinned. "I thought you were waiting for that." Another bite of food; he apparently enjoyed making his clients wait. "Our guy at MGM—the main music producer kid— is named Arthur Freed. He saw the show on Broadway too, liked it, and got his bosses to bribe the rights away from Columbia. Gave them twenty-five Gs extra, I understand, in addition to the hundred and fifty for the play itself. Plus, so they say, MGM traded them Gene Kelly for a picture they want. Anyway, the whole thing just came to Metro, and you know, that's our bread and butter over there. Waldo's been an MGM kid from the get-go."

I flushed happily. *Will this actually be a decent role? Will my friends get to see me on the screen for more than seven seconds?*

Dad, who admittedly enjoyed seeing all the pretty starlets dotting the Hollywood landscape, asked the obvious question. "If Rita Hayworth's out, who's playing the lead now?"

Lew was in a teasing mood. "I guess it's some youngster named Diane Belmont."

A pause. Dad, disappointed, sagged a bit. "Huh. Never heard of her."

My agent grinned as he took a bite of his Caesar salad. "Oh, I think you have. That's just the name she uses on the stage. Her real name's Lucille. You know, Lucille Ball?"

Mom gasped in pleasure. "Oh, she's a stunner! She's the prettiest thing."

My agent snickered. "Well, actually, she was the runner-up. Freed was ready to run down Sunset Boulevard in his skivvies in order to get Lana Turner—in fact, he *had* her all contracted up and everything. But she went and got herself pregnant. So we're going to have a red-headed riot on our hands instead."

"Huh." Dad was fascinated by the gossip grinding through the Hollywood machine. "What kind of story is it?"

Our waitress came over to the table just then to see if we wanted any dessert. Mom gave me a barely visible head shake, which Lew noticed immediately. "Oh, stop it, Mama," he scolded. Then to me, "The agency's buyin', so have anything you want, kiddo."

Mom and Dad ordered the tiramisu, and I asked for a bowl of spumoni ice cream. Baby Dennis burbled happily as he sampled tiny bites of everybody's desserts, and my agent carefully explained the story.

" 'Course, the film version will have some changes, but the basic musical story takes place in a military prep school. Some generic place on the East Coast. Boys, like Darwood here, thirteen, fourteen, fifteen, sixteen, studying to qualify for admission to West Point."

"So that's what Darwood would play?"

"Yup. One of the guys at the school."

"So then what?" Mom took a napkin and wiped my brother's face.

Lew finished his dessert and dabbed at the corners of his mouth as well. "OK. The main boy at the school, Bud—we're getting Tommy Dix, right from the stage play for the role—gets the bright idea to invite movie star Lucille Ball, all the way from Hollywood, to come be his date for the spring prom. Just as a way to show off in front of his friends."

"So she plays *herself* in the film?" Dad wanted to know.

"Yup."

"But why would she do it? I mean, in the story?" Mom was laughing as she asked. "A Hollywood glamour girl going clear across the country to dance with some boy she's never heard of?"

Lew chuckled. "Honey, I look in the mirror and I can answer that question for you. Her publicity agent wants her to do it! Thinks it'd make a great story and jump-start her own film career. 'Hollywood starlet goes cross-country to bring joy and a fluttery heart to one of our brave lads about to ship out for the front.' That kind of thing."

"Gotcha." Dad leaned back in the leatherette booth. "And the whole comedy shtick is 'cause she says Yes and shows up."

"That's it exactly," my agent nodded. "And you see, this Dix kid has already got a girlfriend right there in town. He wrote the mash note only as a joke really, never figuring that Lucille Ball—I mean, come on, *Lucille Ball*?—would say Yes. So now he's got to figure out a way to get his own girl, Helen, out of the way so she doesn't find out he's two-timing her."

The waitress brought the check, and Mr. Sherril shoved it into his jacket pocket. Glancing at his watch, he gulped. "Sorry, folks. I'd love to stay here and run you through the whole story, but I got a two-thirty meeting back at the office." He looked from one of us to the other. "But we're in, right?"

"Well, give me two seconds more," Dad interjected. "I mean, Darwood's one of the boys, OK. But what's the role?"

Lew nodded. "Sure. The part he's up for—this is cute—is called 'Killer.' And the joke is, the character is actually the opposite of what the name suggests. They want someone kind of thin and reedy. In a way, a bit of 'Waldo' still."

He glanced over at me. Since leaving *Our Gang* two years earlier, I had shot up a good five inches or so and now stood around five-three. But I was still rather slight, very smooth cheeked, and with a bit of a professorial aura about me.

Another glance at his watch. "I figure if Waldo here dresses up in an army-type outfit two sizes too large, the casting call will be a piece of cake."

"When is it?" Mom asked. "I'll probably have to drive him; George is in Bakersfield on business the rest of this week."

"Tuesday morning. Right there at MGM." Lew gave me a casual thumbs-up. "They're basically doing all of the cadet roles that morning." He paused. "Look. The reality is, I've already talked to the casting director, and Waldo's essentially in unless he goes in there and wets his pants in front of everyone. It's MGM, they know him, it's a Waldo-type of character; it's a done deal."

"Fantastic." Dad gave me a loving cuff on the upper arm. "What do you say, sport?"

I grinned. "Sure. Cool."

"And how does two hundred and fifty clams a week sound to you?" Lew boasted. "Pretty good pay, huh?"

That made it a very pleasant drive back to the house. My mind was boggling, *A thousand dollars a month? In 1943?*

The screen test turned out to be a perfunctory breeze. The youthful Broadway star, Tommy Dix, was on hand, and he and two buddies had directions to cuff me around a bit. I was supposed to protest weakly but knuckle under at the slightest provocation. We ran through the improvised scene a couple of times, and the stocky casting director nodded. "Yeah, we're good." He clapped me on the back while ticking off one more name on his roster. "You and your mom, go by personnel; they'll have the contract for you there."

I gulped when I discovered that we were all leaving town. The entire story was going to be filmed in Wisconsin, at a place called St. John's Northwestern Military Academy! We were going to be out of state for nearly a month. In fact, I was going to have to miss the first week of my freshman year at high school. Mom helped me pack a suitcase for the train trip; in one corner of my bags, she tucked some homemade goodies.

"I know they'll feed you real well, doll," she managed, almost tearing up, "but that's just to remind you of home."

Dennis bumped into me, pushing a toy car up my leg. "Kenny go bye-bye? Kenny go bye-bye?"

I scooped him up and kissed him on both cheeks. "Yeah. Kenny go bye-bye." I was trying to put on a nonchalant front, but the thought of being away from my parents for three weeks was scary. Work on the *Our Gang* set had been leisurely, a few hours of shooting and plenty of play. We were always home for supper. Now I was going on a train clear across the country and would be sharing a dormitory room with two actors I'd never met.

My friend Carmelo rode out to the depot with Mom to help see me off.

Mom was eternally proud of this publicity shot! But for some reason, Lucille Ball preferred an obscure Cuban band leader named Desi Arnaz.

The train arrived in Delafield on a day that was roaring hot. Two buses took the cast and crew out to the military school, a small but elegant boys' school established in 1884. Years after we shot *Best Foot Forward* on their campus, I read that Hollywood had rented it again for the sinister religious thriller *Damien: Omen II*. Many of the stagehands had arrived ahead of us, and the place was buzzing with celluloid activity.

The academy had agreed to cater the entire shoot using its own cafeteria and staff; of course, St. John's was excited about the great publicity they were going to receive from being in a blockbuster Hollywood musical. Local reporters were milling around, and at dinner that first evening, I caught a glimpse of Lucille Ball's signature red hair as she joked with the Wisconsin media. (Gossip on the train had been that MGM hairdressers had just recently turned her auburn hair into its now flaming hue.) I wondered if I'd have a chance to meet the former Ziegfeld girl in person. The MGM newsletter reported that she was married to some Cuban band leader named Arnaz, but a number of the makeup artists had openly gossiped about the fragility of the marital arrangement. Apparently, Lucy had suffered a miscarriage the previous year, but she appeared the picture of glowing femininity.

Amazingly, the very next morning all of the boys were summoned to a scenic quadrangle in the center of the campus. High atop a metal pole, an American flag was snapping in the stiff August breeze, and the sidewalks were ringed with colorful azaleas that had been quickly planted for the Technicolor musical.

"We're taking a bunch of publicity shots," the photographer announced, "and the boss wants to get 'em out of the way now before major shooting begins. Miss Ball, thank you for taking time."

The perky redhead cackled her trademark laugh and then joked, "Well, fellas, you're all about ten years too young for me, but you know, in Hollywood we bend the rules. Who knows? I might just pick one of you big men out for my very own." Her voice had a bit of scratchiness from the perennial cigarette she had in one hand, but in the morning sunlight, she was the picture of loveliness.

Years later, as my family and I watched old *I Love Lucy* reruns on television, I could never forget how *flat* those black-and-white pictures were in contrast to the vivid color of that morning at St. John's. All of us cadets were smartly dressed in our Army blue dress uniforms, replete with neckties and caps. The photographer got us into a semicircle around our beloved femme fatale and began snapping furiously. The local media was there as well, of course, and the chorus of clicking shutters sounded like an invasion of locusts.

I sucked in my breath when the publicity director called my name.

"Darwood, they tell me we want a shot of just you and Miss Ball, arm in arm, walking down this sidewalk right here." He pointed to a spot about fifteen yards away. "Just walk toward us nice and slowlike. Try to look like a 'Killer.' " He snorted a half laugh.

Lucille, her makeup still intact despite the building midmorning heat, found her spot and took my arm with a smile. The knot of male actors whooped; in her high heels and hat, she towered a good six inches over me. "Good luck, Killer!" one of them hollered. "Better hike her over to those steps if you plan on kissing her!" I blushed a deep crimson, but my walking partner emitted a cheerful laugh. "It's a date, honeybunch. I'll meet you there at midnight tonight." She gave my arm a squeeze. "They tell me you were in the *Gang* for a while." She paused in midstep, rebalancing a small dog that for some reason they had perched on her left shoulder.

"Uh-huh." It was all I could manage with my stomach doing flip-flops.

The photographer snapped off four or five quick shots and gave us the high sign. "I got it." He turned to look behind him. "Next!"

Our cadet scenes weren't scheduled to be taped until the weekend, so all the guys had a chance to relax and explore the campus. Most of the time, though, we hung around in the main assembly hall, which MGM had converted into a professional soundstage. All of us were buzzing over the fact that Harry James and his orchestra had been booked to do all of the music. A thin, dapper man with a pencil mustache, he was one of the hottest horn players in the country in the early 1940s. We eagerly lined the walls of the gym, out of camera range, as he and his band belted their way through sizzling hits such as "Two O' Clock Jump" and various rollicking show tunes. His personal trumpet playing on "Flight of the Bumblebee" was beyond belief. A main theme of the film was going to be "The Three B's"—June Allyson and her two costars were on-screen to showcase the barrel roll, boogie-woogie, and the blues. There was a lot of toe-tapping on the sidelines, and I reveled in the crisp professionalism of the musicians as they blared through the requisite songs over and over again for the rolling cameras. A clever staff writer, working on copy for the film's theatrical trailer, borrowed from the military theme and announced that Harry James was "the world's greatest *jive* bomber."

Interestingly, most of the music for the Broadway show had been composed by Hugh Martin, a seasoned veteran who followed up his success by scoring *Meet Me in St. Louis* in 1944. Years later, I was thrilled to read, he became a devout Seventh-day Adventist Christian and wrote new spiritual lyrics to his greatest hit, "Have Yourself a Merry Little Christmas."

Early the following week, we got the call to assemble to begin shooting some of our scenes. My main shot, one of the first in the film, involved several of the guys harassing me over some bed mattresses I had just lugged into the library, where all of our visiting ladies would be staying. Irving Brecher and Fred Finklehoffe had scripted some funny lines for the cadets to use, and I assumed a cowering pose as Tommy Dix and the others razzed me about doing my job. Didn't I have any school spirit? The script called for me to grumble, "I hate school spirit. I hate dances. I hate girls. I wish they'd draft me!"

Most scenes required just a few takes, and I remember being assigned to pretend I was blowing notes into a massive tuba during one of the early musical numbers. I wondered if MGM had borrowed *Our Gang*'s Mr. Hatley to do the actual playing.

Of course, being right there on campus and with scripts lying around all over the place, it was easy enough to dope out the main story even though MGM was randomly filming scenes out of order in order to be more efficient. Lucille Ball surprises the entire academy by showing up at the prom dance, and Tommy Dix is fighting two frantic battles at once. He has to diplomatically shoo his girlfriend, Helen, off to the sidelines so she doesn't find out. Furthermore, he has to persuade the faculty of Winsocki Military Institute that Miss Ball is a legitimate and appropriate date; the stuffy institution doesn't take kindly to shenanigans involving red-headed sirens from the West Coast.

Naturally, every guy in the place is eager to take Lucy for a midnight stroll in the moonlight, so the story is packed with whistles and masculine plots. One of the main gags has so many eager fans grabbing for a souvenir piece of her ballroom gown that Lucy ends up clad (still modestly) in about half of what she arrived wearing. The climactic comedy scene has the star, Tommy Dix, his furious girlfriend, and half the gang of fellows all hiding in a closet. "A madcap scene reminiscent of the Marx Brothers," read an Internet review posted many decades later. During the prom itself, they assigned me—as the resident nerd—to be the coat check kid and keep track of all the ladies' furs. Not many chances for an Oscar nomination there.

It was enjoyable for me to later notice how no-name stars from *Best Foot Forward* ended up with substantial careers. One youthful B actor was named Gil Stratton; he did some stray bits of acting here and there, but later carved out a hugely successful niche for himself as a sportscaster for CBS in Los Angeles. But the surprise star of the show was a rather plump, four-ten actress named Nancy Walker, who came to the film right from her showbiz debut in the New York stage version. Cheerfully embracing her part as the ugly duckling, she was a talented part of the boogie-woogie trio. Better yet were her self-deprecating bits of humor about her lack of popularity. Late in the film, while the band is stomping out yet another hit, she moans about how not a single cadet has invited her out onto the dance floor. "For everyone else it's a dance," she sighs. "For me it's a concert." Shaking her head in fake despair, she concludes, "I'd hang myself, but I got a dentist appointment on Tuesday." It didn't surprise me at all when she landed a lucrative long-term contract in commercials as Rosie the waitress, who for twenty years used Bounty paper towels, "the Quicker Picker-Upper." And of course, in the 1970s, she earned millions as Ida Morgenstern, Valerie Harper's mother on the CBS hit *Rhoda*.

The closing moments of the film have her sitting in the reviewing stands as all of the cadets parade past in full dress uniform and carrying our rifles. One of the shortest actors on the field, I'm trudging along when Nancy points to me. "There he is," she says to her friend. "There's my fellow. That little guy."

Her companion can scarcely hide her amazement. "You mean Killer?"

"Sure," she says defensively. "We're going steady." (That was news to me.)

"But he's only thirteen," the other girl hoots.

Nancy is undeterred. "By the time he's eighteen, he'll get used to me!"

All during the month-long shoot, the thing that startled my barely teen ears was the language that permeated the movie set. For three-plus seasons back home, *Our Gang* producers had been scrupulously protective of us; the grips and lighting guys were under strict order to keep things kosher on the set. Here in Wisconsin, swearwords and obscene oaths punctuated every mishap. An assistant technician dropped a tray filled with expensive pancake makeup, filling the dressing room with an expensive powdery mist. The controller barked at her angrily, throwing in several epithets that shocked me.

Late that same night, as I walked up to my dorm room on the fourth floor, I passed a parlor where six or seven film executives were huddled around a table. Someone had draped a bedspread over it, and the brown cloth was covered with an astounding mound of dollar bills and silver coins. I watched in fascinated awe as the men fingered their playing cards and dumped poker bets into the center of the action.

Back home, I had been trying to spend just a couple of minutes right at bedtime at least whispering a teenaged prayer. I wasn't one for kneeling by the side of my bed—for sure, not in *my* family—but it had become a comforting habit to me to simply whisper my anxieties to God and ask Him to bless and protect my parents. But there in the cramped conditions of my St. John's room, prayer seemed impossible. In the cafeteria, I once thought about at least mumbling an internal prayer of thanks for the hearty breakfasts they were serving, but my roommates crowded around with bawdy jokes, and I shrugged away my pangs of conscience. Sunday School and Bible verses were part of my distant California life; matters of the kingdom would have to wait until we wrapped on this picture.

It was more than a week later before they drafted the entire cast to parade up to the reviewing stands where Lucy and the generals were sitting and to belt out the show-stopping theme song, "Buckle Down, Winsocki!" At great expense, the MGM people had covered over the name, St. John's Northwestern Military Academy, substituting the stage name so popularized in the Broadway play. I was an anonymous face in the crowd, but I got a rush of adrenaline as we sang and danced our way through the final moments of what we hoped would be an Oscar-winning hit.

Stagehands were already tearing down the elaborate sets and disassembling the huge overhead klieg lights as June Allyson and Lucille Ball came down the line, giving each of the B actors a hug. I remember easing up onto my tiptoes as Lucy approached me.

"You were just swell, sweetie," she purred, probably for the tenth time in as many minutes. "We had fun, didn't we? I hope this thing makes ten million dollars."

"Yes, ma'am." I had mentally rehearsed this moment for the entire week, and I came out with the smart line that had been spinning around in my mind. "I think I'd give ten million dollars to be six inches taller right now."

Lucy roared with laughter and squeezed me again, giving me a generous kiss right where it counted. "You devil," she scolded. "I guess you're a lover, not a killer."

I grinned as she winked and moved away. At that moment, I felt very much the adult star, part of a sophisticated world where clever lines and droll banter would get a man from a good movie role to a better one, from the B list to the coveted inner circle where the stars hung out.

But on the long train ride home, my mind kept returning to Carmelo and his parents and my friends at church. To Grandpa Kite and his Adventist heritage and prayers on my behalf. In my suitcase, I had my complimentary eight-by-ten glossy, showing me arm in arm with one of Hollywood's leading ladies. I had a grand in my pocket and—finally—a big movie on my résumé. "Darwood Kaye. 'Killer.' *Best Foot Forward*, MGM, 1943." I had given my agent something substantial to boast about to his many vaunted connections.

And Grandpa, well, what did he have? I remembered with a bit of shame the edgy conversations, the countless crude sex jokes I'd heard repeated ad nauseam there in the gymnasium. I realized I had been stained by working on this film; there was no denying it. And Grandpa had his place of noble purpose *away* from all that. He had a life of service that moved people toward the possibility of eternity, toward holiness and a kind of purity that I somehow valued all the more now that I had glimpsed the other side in more stark and seamy detail.

As the train crept into Union Station at eleven thirty on Friday night, I accepted Dad's welcoming hug with feelings of empty confusion.

Chapter Fourteen

FINAL CREDITS

"Watch it, Sport!"

Two varsity swimmers almost skidded on the wet pavement surrounding the swimming pool at Hollywood High. It was a late April afternoon, and our varsity athletes were late getting to a scheduled meet against the El Monte and Glendale teams.

I had transitioned easily enough to my new life in high school. Even though *Best Foot Forward* had done a decent box office business in Los Angeles, it just wasn't the kind of film most high school students bothered to go see, so within weeks of registering I was glad to be just a normal kid. I was a bit young to be a freshman; I turned fourteen a few days after school began and I felt dwarfed by some of the varsity basketball and football athletes who roamed the hallways.

Before the first semester ended, Mr. Gergen had spotted my flair for writing and assigned me to work on the school newspaper. I was thrilled when the student editor asked me if I minded writing some sports stories about the junior varsity squads.

"Are you kidding?" I grinned. "That'd be perfect." I followed our basketball teams around Southern California, attending most of the home games and a few of the road ones as well, creatively drafting prose that glorified our victories and made humorous excuses for our many losses. Once spring arrived, I enjoyed Thursday afternoons in the bleachers at our junior varsity ball field and tried to craft reports that were more exciting than the usual boxes of scores that sometimes clogged up the sports pages of student papers.

I hadn't gotten into swimming meets yet, but Steve, our editor, wanted me to see if I could "make a splash" for the paper, as he groaningly put it. So that's where I was.

It was a difficult chore, because Glendale had brought a busload of elite speedsters who were almost lapping our own athletes. Watching four races, I dolefully noticed that we'd gotten only a single fourth-place finish and that was because the visitors had been penalized with two false starts. Scribbling down some cryptic notes in my pad, I gingerly stepped around the gathering puddles of chlorinated water and began mentally composing my lead.

I was just about to the exit gate when a sudden burst of angry sound grabbed me back. Two swimmers, still just in their trunks, had come to blows and were tugging each other toward a grassy area lining the west side of the Olympic-sized pool.

"You dirty %#&@!" I heard an epithet as the juniors grunted heavily, neither one able to gain an advantage. Several kids gathered around, wide-eyed at the slippery grappling and blood-red eyes.

A coach, standing in the doorway of the nearby gym, blew his whistle and began striding toward the melee. All at once, the shorter of the two swimmers, a kid named Tony, pulled away. "Hey, hey, hey," he began. "I . . ."

He backed out of range and buried his face in his hands for a moment. The taller swimmer took a step forward, but Tony held up a hand. "No," he said. "No. I'm sorry, man. My fault."

His antagonist hesitated, his chest still heaving. I was about twenty feet away, dead in my tracks. Would the fisticuffs resume? The coach,

Scotty Beckett and I, both Our Gang *alumni, get a few more dollars in a Barbara Stanwyck B movie from Warner Brothers entitled* My Reputation. *Mine wasn't going much of anywhere at this rate.*

seeing the cease-fire, waited to see whether he still needed to intervene.

The dark-haired swimmer who had backed away looked around and then proffered a hand. "Look," he said. "I shouldn't have gone after you. I don't know why I did that." A long beat. "I apologize."

I was agog, watching the surreal moment. Dustups were common on the sports field; football, of course, had routine eye pokes and fits of temper. Basketball players had to be plopped down on the bench for fighting; suspensions were common in high-school sports. But I had never before seen a fight after a swim meet and certainly not between teammates.

The older athlete, his face a study in turmoil, finally nodded. "Buzz off," he said shortly. He spurned the proffered handshake and stiffly walked away. A couple of senior guys who had seen the whole thing edged over to him. "Man, you shoulda decked him. Are you kidding?"

"Go to hell."

My grip tightened on my pencil. I figured this was a great story, but now was not the time. I made a mental note to quietly dig into it later.

The next afternoon, after some surreptitious checking, I noticed that Tony had study hall during fourth period. I eased over to him in the library, thankful that he was sitting alone at a table.

"I saw what happened at the pool yesterday afternoon," I said without preamble, hoping he would talk to me.

He chewed on his lip, eyeing me. "So?"

"Man, that was a wild fight. Looked like you guys were both pretty steamed."

"Yeah. I guess."

I had my pad of paper and pencil in my left hand, beneath the table, hoping he'd let his guard down. "So what was it all about? You're on the same team. I mean, did he beat you or something?"

Tony carefully closed his geometry textbook and looked at me. "You're that kid—you write for the paper. Right?"

"Yeah."

He shook his head. "So I don't want to tell you. Me bein' in a fight and then having it in the paper. My folks would kill me. Coach too."

I sighed. "Well, what about, like, off the record?"

"What's that?"

"Just tell me and I won't print it." I had quickly learned the essential rules of Journalism 101.

He shook his head. "Nah. You're a liar, man. You'd write it up."

"No." I held up both hands, and carefully pushed the notepad away. "Swear to God. Off the record is off the record. 'Sides, if I broke the rules and printed something you said I couldn't, I'd be booted off the paper."

"Seriously?" He brightened. "That's kind of . . ." His voice trailed off as he looked me over. I was still a rather slight and unassuming-looking kid, and he obviously hadn't gone to *Our Gang* film festivals.

"Come on," I pressed. "Man, I walked all the way over here from algebra just to find you."

His features relaxed. "Well, I guess, then. That other guy, Will, spent the last three weeks calling me names, and I finally snapped is all."

"What kind of names?"

Another pause. "Oh—goody boy. Jesus' little helper. Stuff like that."

"What do you mean?"

Tony picked up a pencil and slowly traced a lazy circle on the back of his paper while I waited. "Just 'cause my folks and I go to church and everything."

I wrinkled up my nose. "So? I go to church. I mean, some of the time. Why's that a big headline?"

"I don't know." He shook his head. "He doesn't apparently. And he knows I do. And that was enough to make him mad."

I pondered that. "OK. Well, then—I mean, all of a sudden, you backed away. Said you were sorry. Was the fight your fault?" I was dying to take some notes, but I'd made a promise and I intended to keep it.

Tony leaned closer. "You know what? It's my fault in the sense that I . . . was in a fight. Whose fault was it? I don't know. But I'm a Christian and I can't be in fights."

My mind reeled. In fourteen years of life, in the movies and in real life, I had never bumped into a kid who said such a thing. *I'm a Chris-*

tian and it impacts my life in such-and-such a way.

"Are you serious?" I found it hard to catch my voice. "Just like that?"

He seemed ill at ease by the question, but he didn't back away from his assertion. "Yeah. Sure." He shook his head. "Christians aren't supposed to fight; we're supposed to be peacemakers. That's in the Beatitudes, man."

I vaguely remembered hearing something about that when Carmelo and I had attended a Friday-evening folk concert at his church the previous Thanksgiving. I recalled something about the Sermon on the Mount and the book of Matthew, and the youth speaker describing how the teachings of Christ had changed the world. But here before me was a kid, just two years older than I was, who had the guts to walk away from a fight and then tell a student news reporter that Jesus Christ had some kind of claim on his daily behavior.

"Wow," I said at last. "Wow."

We fell into an odd-fellow friendship, seeing that he was two grades ahead of me. He made the varsity swim team his senior year, and occasionally he'd drive his own car to meets and then give me a ride home. It was fun to stop on the way and split a pizza, and he was unabashed about bowing his head and saying grace right in front of the waiters. Grandpa thought it was great and encouraged the friendship in his letters to me. "Be sure to tell that Tony fellow hello," he would add at the close of his monthly notes. "I love a man of spiritual courage . . . so glad to hear you're choosing to turn your life in that direction as well."

Many years later, I read a fascinating account of how Christian author C. S. Lewis was finally compelled to abandon his atheism. Despite his determination to stay clear of heaven's kingdom, God was pursuing and wooing him with logic and a sense of his deep need. Late in his autobiography, *Surprised by Joy,* he entitles a chapter

"Checkmate" and wryly observes, "My Adversary began to make His final moves."[1] Looking back, I can see how the Lord invaded Hollywood High and moved His divine chess pieces into position for an all-out assault on my spiritual indecision.

I didn't know how abrupt of a life turn it would be, but I finally accepted Tony's invitation to attend church. Carmelo's family had suddenly picked up and moved back to San Diego, so I had been thinking that I ought to find a new place to attend. Tony picked me up that weekend and we drove over what seemed to be familiar territory. "Are you serious?" I gaped, as he wheeled into the Adventist church parking lot. "Man, I've been to this place before."

"You have not."

"Sure have." I pointed. "My grandpa used to bring me to this exact church when he was out here visiting after my grandma died." I couldn't believe it. Tony's church family was friendly, and they had an active Van Nuys youth group. I still remembered the names of a few of the kids. We sometimes went to the beach for Friday evening campfires. Tony knew a few guitar chords, and the girls teased him about making the entire group hold a long note while he laboriously switched from a C to a G7 chord in the middle of "Michael, Row Your Boat Ashore." Pastor Rhodes seemed genuinely delighted to have me back and let me know how welcome I was.

Long uncluttered months at Hollywood High drifted along without Lew Sherril phoning or coming by. My stint on the Lucille Ball film seemed to indicate that I was pretty rigidly typecast as a perennial Waldo; the only roles I was going to get would involve glasses and beefier guys pushing me around. I didn't mind that particularly, but wondered if I had any chance of a Hollywood career with traces of testosterone in it. The summer after my sophomore year, he did get me a week of work on a story called *Kansas City Kitty*. It was a smallish musical drama involving a piano teacher, and I dutifully

Another still from My Reputation. *I'm standing at the far left; Scotty gets the spot-light.*

handed Mom the few dollars it brought in. I also had an eyeblink role in a World War II thriller entitled *Submarine Alert,* with some FBI sleuthing and American ships being sunk. I remember wearing a set of radio headphones and tracking some sinister signals. But again, it was the kind of role where if you bent over to pick up a piece of popcorn off the floor, you wouldn't have seen me at all.

"You gonna go see it?" Tony teased, as we rode to a big gospel quartet convention down in Long Beach. He had a little car his older brother had bequeathed to him when he joined the army, and I usually handed him a buck to help with the gas whenever we went here or there.

I shrugged. "Nah. My part was so little I'd have trouble telling you where to look."

A laugh. "Man, Ken, you're just on a meteoric trajectory."

My parents always accepted my church-oriented field trips without question. They'd ask if I enjoyed myself and then drop the subject. Most Sabbaths now, I was gone for several hours to Tony's church, and they shrugged it off. Every night before dropping off to sleep, I thanked the Lord that their marriage seemed to be on a solid footing again and that my little brother Dennis was a healthy kid. Once or twice, he tagged along with us on our weekend rides to the church in Van Nuys; Tony and I would drop him off with the other four-year-old boys and girls in the kindergarten department and then study the Sabbath School lesson with our teen friends. Tony was a high-school graduate by now, and Pastor Rhodes plied him with suggestions about various Adventist colleges he recommended.

The summer before my senior year of high school, Lew sent me for several casting calls, and I came up empty in all of them. The war in the Pacific had just ended, and Southern California was flooded with returning GIs. Plenty of them, hardened, with the appealing enigma of battle scars and a tan earned on the beaches of Iwo Jima, were showing up at MGM and Columbia for tryouts, and a slim high-school student like me wasn't going to find many roles.

"Just be patient," Lew kept advising me. "I've got my eyes and ears open. We'll get you back in the biz."

I had just turned sixteen and proudly tucked my brand-new driver's license in my wallet, when Tony showed me a handbill from church. "What do you think?" he asked me as we split a plate of french fries at a greasy diner not far from the high school. He was now attending a nearby trade school, but stopped by to say Hi every week or so.

I scanned the copy. Pastor Rhodes had arranged for a missionary friend of his—some guy named McComas—to come out to California and hold a series of teaching meetings in Van Nuys. Because the church was too small to hold the anticipated crowd, they had rented a huge circus tent and were planning to invite the public to come study the Bible in an intensive series of studies that were going to last for all of October.

"I don't know," I responded. "That's a lot of church, mister. I'm not in that big a rush to get into heaven." I didn't have a particularly heavy load of classes at Hollywood High, but I was still writing stories for the paper and trying to capture the attention of Vivian, a junior I'd met in my chemistry class the previous spring.

Tony tucked the flier inside the front cover of my English textbook. "Well, think about it." He dipped the last of the fries in ketchup and chewed on it thoughtfully. "I think this would be good for you, man. I mean, you coming to church with me now and then is great. But this would really immerse you in all the teachings of the Bible. Get you ready for—I don't know—even getting baptized. Or whatever."

Despite the many months of visiting, both at Carmelo's church and now with Tony in Van Nuys, the idea of baptism had never really been broached before. The youth group, despite knowing I was essentially a permanent visitor, had embraced me warmly and made me feel right at home even without my getting dunked. And of course, Mom and Dad were very settled in our family lifestyle of respectful secularism.

Tony walked me out to where my car was parked. Dad had dipped into a bit of our leftover MGM money and helped me buy a little Chevy with a few minor scrapes on the rear fender. I leaned out the window before pulling away and said to him, "Well, at least this weekend we can go check it out. If we like it, who knows?"

Friday afternoon Mom assigned me to go down to the local supermarket and pick up a long list of groceries and to take Dennis with me. Now that I could drive, I was happy to do errands for her, and my towheaded little brother chattered happily as he pestered me to visit the candy section. I responded with monosyllabic answers, but I was deep in thought as we roamed the aisles.

There were several realities inviting consideration during this time of decision. First of all, I had to admit, I *liked* church—and singing and sermons. Those were enjoyable things to me. I savored even the casual friendships I had now in Van Nuys, the pretty Adventist girls who talked about Jesus in between campfire songs, the woman from Mexico who got up and read Bible verses before Pastor Rhodes's sermons. I even liked the sermons—the pastor's teachings from the pulpit made sense to me and were filled with positive stories. When he made a strong assertion about some Bible truth, he always seemed to have an abundance of texts that backed up what he was saying. Overall, my personality type was that I found being a part of the Christian world a pleasant and encouraging thing.

The second reality, though, was that I was just admiring all of this from a secure vantage point. I had never made a commitment. I knew Mom had left her childhood Adventist faith and that what I was doing now was a long step away from what Grandpa Kite envisioned for me. I was a safe observer, like the youngster who spent a dime to watch *Our Gang* activities up on a theater screen but wasn't personally a part of the action. My friend Tony had bluntly said to me after the fracas at the swimming pool: "I'm a Christian. My allegiance to this faith, to this *Man*, orders my life by these heavenly principles." I still wanted that and was drawn to it, but the moment of decision had never come. That wasn't anyone's fault but my own; I was still living in two worlds and keeping my Hollywood options open.

The third thing I had to weigh was my career. Ever since 1937, and it was now late 1945, I had been only Waldo. Erudite and a bit emaciated, with those eternal glasses perched on my nose so I could look down with élan on other people. I still dreamed of someday landing

Even as we got older, the studio was required to dish out our daily dose of the three Rs. Our schoolmarm on Our Gang was the incomparable Fern Carter. Here we're cajoled by a Mrs. Mullen. I'm on the left side, pretending to study.

a huge role and becoming a leading man—what member of the Screen Actor's Guild didn't?—but even if I was forever typecast as a bookworm, it was a wonderfully lucrative and ego-stoking living. Casting directors were always telling their people: "I need a fat guy. Get so-and-so." "I'm looking for a bald, weak-willed accountant. Doesn't Mr. X always do those for us? See if he's in town." Hattie McDaniel pulled in seven hundred dollars a week because of her willingness to always wear a maid's outfit when acting in the movies. At the 1939 Oscar ceremony, they probably handed her a gold statuette for one hand and a mop for the other, but she flourished even within that narrowly defined and demeaning niche. Should I do the same?

Tony and I began going to the Van Nuys tent meetings that Friday evening. There were several hundred people there, and I remember sitting in the back row and watching with interest. A quartet from Pacific Union College did several numbers, and I enjoyed the close harmony and the exuberance of the crowd. The visiting evangelist, Pastor J. W. McComas, had a dynamic delivery but was also very genial and personable. Both Tony and I shook his hand after the meeting, said Hi to his wife, and promised we'd be back the following night.

Mom was in the living room, listening to the radio as we pulled up, and she nodded as I told her we'd enjoyed our evening. "Help yourselves to some root beer," she said. Tony and I leaned against the front fender of his car, sipping our ice-cold drinks and discussing the evening message.

And for the next month, I diligently finished my homework during my daily study hall so that I could attend the meetings. Tony had a night class on Mondays and Wednesdays, so I would carefully motor over to the tent meeting by myself, enjoying the cool October air in my face and the syncopated jazz music filling the Chevy with good cheer. The Bible topics were carefully arranged to give newcomers like me an overall sense of God's plan for His lost race of children. We studied the effects of sin, the Daniel prophecies of a soon-coming Savior, the story of Calvary, Bible promises about resurrection and life after death, the doctrine of grace, and the Second Coming. I had a little Bible Grandpa Kite had sent me years before, and I carefully marked it with red underlining so I could find my favorite verses again.

Often as Pastor McComas preached, I would catch myself thinking, *Huh. I wonder how I would have phrased that?* I supposed it was my training as an actor that triggered my critical presentation skills, but I sometimes drove home envisioning myself in a similar role, finding new ways to make the Bible and the invitation of Jesus attractive to other people.

The last Friday evening of the series, Tony was away, and there was a huge traffic tie-up that made me late. The tent was filled to overflowing, and I ended up in the very back of the huge tent, perched on the edge of a table where Pastor Rhodes had stacks of giveaway books about tithe paying and heaven. I was still rather slight of build, even as a senior—I was barely seventeen—and my feet dangled lazily as I drank in the message. Pastor McComas was passionate in his description of the grace of God, the overpowering hunger that Jesus had to bring us back into His family.

"There was a cost," he reminded us, "when Jesus came to this broken world. Think of that cost. Jesus was admired in heaven; He was loved; He was worshiped. His Father loved Him and He loved His Father. Focus on that. How would it feel for me or for you to be torn away from your closest friends and family and have to spend thirty-three years in a world filled with hate and war and loneliness? And to do that, not for yourself, but for *others?*"

I wasn't usually one for sentimentality; but there in that tent, as the cool October breezes slipped in through the gaps in the canvas and brushed my face, I felt the trace of tears. What this kind believer was describing, I wanted. I wanted to be a full part of this movement that embraced Calvary.

A woman named Hilda began softly playing on the organ as the pastor wrapped up his appeal. Men and women began to move toward the front, carefully stepping over the long extension cords that ringed the platform. I saw high school kids moving to the altar. A few elementary-age girls were standing on the left side; one of them was dabbing at her eyes as her classmates embraced her.

I didn't know what to do. In my heart, I had long felt that someday and some way, I would join Grandpa Kite in becoming a Christian.

At least the goofy glasses are gone here in Submarine Alert, *a smallish picture from Paramount.*

Everything I had heard from him and now in this tent confirmed that it was what I wanted.

At the same time, a resolute part of me still envisioned the moment when my name would be the first one listed in a big Hollywood film. I still wanted to do *one* story in which my lines of dialogue would be central to the tale, where my on-screen acting would compel the story line and touch people's lives. I didn't care so much about an Oscar award, but the lure of staying in the game, seeing how far this glittery town could take me, was still very strong. I wanted to escape from my Waldo straitjacket one time and discover my highest cinematic potential.

The tearing at my soul was a shuddering, almost physical sensation. The organ was still playing as the two kingdoms beckoned. Was it possible to do both of these things? Could I give my life to Jesus

Christ and still seek that elusive top billing down on Sunset Boulevard? For eight seasons in Hollywood's minor leagues, the answer had been No. And it wasn't simply the vulgarity of the town, the cynical scripts, and the voluptuous females who were ever present on major studio lots. It was more a matter of *self*: this was a place where your own ambitions had to occupy first place or you were finished.

As if watching a playback reel, my mind reviewed the projects I had enjoyed since arriving in Los Angeles. The innocent bit parts as a youngster in grown-up films, then the fame of being in Hal Roach's franchise—even as a backup act to Alfalfa and Spanky. Now the heady tidbits of screen time here and there in projects such as *Best Foot Forward*. I realized that I had spent my entire childhood on the edge of both of these worlds: minor success in the movies and a noncommittal, *safe* visitor's tour of the city of God.

All at once, despite my conflicting feelings, my feet hit the grassy sod, and I was walking to the front. Tony wasn't with me; my mom and dad were home in their Hollywood bungalow, listening to Sinatra on the hi-fi. And here I was, making a decision without fully having settled what that decision was. All I know is I was standing underneath that cross.

Pastor McComas said a brief prayer for all of us, and as he said Amen, I felt a light touch. It was our Van Nuys minister, Pastor Rhodes. "This is beautiful!" he said to me, his eyes warm. "I'm so glad, Ken."

I mumbled something, and he added, "Where's Tony?"

"Couldn't make it."

He motioned me toward the back of the tent, and we retreated to a quiet corner. People were milling toward the exit, fishing in their purses and pockets for their car keys. "Do your folks know?" he asked.

I shook my head. "Well, they know I've been coming here a lot. To these meetings. But not about this."

"Huh." He put a fatherly hand on my shoulder and gave me an affectionate squeeze. "Well, Jo and I are just thrilled with your decision, Ken. This is wonderful." He noticed his wife walking past, and he motioned for her to join us. She was a small, light-haired woman with laugh lines around her eyes. "Honey, Ken just came forward tonight."

"I saw." She gave me a nice hug and a pat on my upper arm. "What a wonderful night this has been. I've never seen anything like this."

"Do you feel like you're ready to be baptized at our last meeting?" The bulletin had announced a concluding baptism for Sunday night, but I had been too mesmerized by the sermon to notice.

"Uh . . . boy, I don't know." My reluctance was written all over my face, I'm sure. He noticed immediately. "Your folks?"

I hesitated. "Yeah. I guess. Plus . . ." I shook my head in confusion.

There was a pause. The crowd was thinning out now, and two deacons were putting away the big slide projector and the screen. I could hear the faint hum of the portable generator outside the tent and the low rumble of cars pulling out onto the highway.

"Look," Pastor Rhodes said. "It's still kind of early out. Why don't you wait just a few minutes while I get things locked up here? You can pop over to the house and let's see if Mrs. Rhodes will let us steal some ice cream out of the freezer. If there are problems in the way, I'll bet you fifty dollars we can solve them together."

I managed a grin. Even though all of this had happened so quickly, this felt like the right thing. I wanted to drive home knowing what I was going to do with my life.

Over a heaping bowl of chocolate ice cream, I openly described my adventures in the film business, starting with *Our Gang* and my first roles as Waldo eight years earlier.

"So you were a pretty big player?" Pastor Rhodes seemed impressed.

"Oh, I don't know about that," I replied. "But, yeah. I was right there with Alfalfa and Spanky."

"I knew you had done a bit of that," he conceded. "Seems like Tony mentioned it once. But I didn't realize what a big deal it was. And how important."

I was grateful that he was willing to acknowledge the substance of all I had achieved. I took another bite of ice cream and felt it melting on my tongue. Pastor Rhodes's wife slipped up behind me and put one more scoop in my bowl. I began to protest, but she showed me the empty container. "Do me a favor and finish it." I grinned.

My pastor finished his dessert and pushed his bowl to the side. "Let me ask you this, Ken. Is it possible for you, as a Christian, to succeed in the movie business at the same time? In your heart, do you feel you can do both?"

"No." Now I didn't hesitate. I had already come to understand that the Adventist community resisted the coarseness of Hollywood films and discouraged its members from attending. And I was in a better position than most to know why. Ever since being on the set of *Best Foot Forward* in Wisconsin, I had been forced to face up to the reality that the kind of film career I was in could not honestly coexist with the claims of Jesus. I was lying to myself if I thought so. I simply could not be on a movie set and pray and witness for the Lord. Again, it wasn't so much that Hollywood was a hostile environment—although the obscene jokes, the casual sex, and the large poker pots were a daily reality. It was just that this town was decidedly and permanently secular. I wasn't a strong enough kind of guy to carry my Bible into MGM and put it on the table of my dressing room where everyone could see it. I knew myself well enough to confess the impossibility of this dual life.

Rhodes's voice softened. "So you are having to make a very painful choice here."

"Uh-huh." I pulled a piece of paper out of my back pocket. "Look at this."

I showed him a paystub from a picture I had just finished shooting sometime earlier. It had been filmed across town at Warner Brothers, a love story entitled *My Reputation*. It had starred Barbara Stanwyck, one of the screen sirens of 1945, and Lew had managed to get me into the project because Scotty Beckett, Alfalfa's predecessor, had been given a good role as the heroine's son. I had played the part of Bill "Droopy" Hawks, with a few decent lines of dialogue and several minutes of screen time. I had been offered a total of two hundred fifty dollars for a week of work, but for some reason the American release had been pushed back almost two years. Being a war story, Warner Brothers had sent preview copies out for the troops in Europe to enjoy while holding it back here at home. With the film's release being delayed clear into 1946, the last installment of my pay had just come in a few days earlier.

"Huh." Pastor Rhodes looked it over. "And you're wondering if you can pass this up. In the future, I mean." He fingered the slip of paper with its enticing numbers. "Was it a good story?"

I shrugged. "This lady's a widow and she falls in love with a guy in the army. There's some scene where they're skiing up at Tahoe, and he has to sleep on the couch that night." I hadn't looked at the script for nearly a year, but the story's amoral tone and the double entendre of the love triangles were obvious even to a teenager like me.

Pastor Rhodes looked me in the eye. "Here's what I think you're struggling with, Ken. Tell me if I'm wrong." He set the paystub down and pointed to it. "This is nice, sure. You like it; your folks like it."

"Yeah."

"Now you wonder if it's worth it to leave this behind in order to be a Christian."

I nodded my head. That was my crossroads; I knew it. Hollywood or God's kingdom. Clark Gable's world or Grandpa Kite's.

"What do you think?" He asked the question softly.

I began to describe my earlier nagging itch. Could I walk away from these little roles, where I said three sentences and heard the word "Cut" just a few seconds after the word "Action"? Yes. I had enjoyed eight years of bit parts, but I didn't have to do that forever. I could leave Waldo behind.

"But what about this?" I leaned forward and tried to pour out my heart. "I know I'm not the world's greatest actor, but I'm good. I got into *Our Gang* when a lot of other kids didn't. When Mr. McDonald told me to act this way or that way, I could do it in one take. I could learn my lines. I didn't flub up on the set."

"Sure." Pastor Rhodes seemed intensely interested. "You were a pro in the business."

"So here's the thing," I concluded. "What if I stick around and really give it my best shot? What if I'm just one year away from that big role where I'm, you know, the lead character? Mr. Sherril tells me he's talking to this guy and that; there are big deals happening all the time. I don't have anything yet, but he's always saying, 'Just hang on. Just hang on. I'm getting it all together.' " The clumsily articulated dream sat there in the air before us, verbally suspended as a wall against my newfound Christian convictions.

"That would be something," the pastor conceded. "Every now and then a kid like you gets clear to the top. Makes a million dollars."

"Yeah." I mentally viewed some of the Beverly Hills mansions Mom, Dad, and I sometimes saw on our Saturday afternoon drives throughout town. Dad loved to slowly wend his way through Rodeo Drive, ogling all of the palatial estates overlooking the twinkling lights of Hollywood. We weren't going to get there on bit parts from Republic Pictures and three seconds in *Gone With the Wind,* but actors like me were always waiting for their big moment. Paradise was never more than one casting call away.

The pastor leaned forward, his blue eyes close to mine. "Ken," he said softly, "let me give you something to think about."

"Sure."

He paused, formulating his thoughts. "A man in your position has to weigh his opportunities and then make a choice bathed in wisdom. You could act in one bad film or some story that offends Hollywood, and have your career go up in smoke right now. Am I right?"

I nodded. That was reality too.

"OK," he went on. "Let's presume that your highest dream comes true. You could get one lucky role, and all of a sudden, be the next John Wayne or Robert Montgomery. Let's say you do."

I waited.

"And you have this life. Limos. Big house. Pretty wife. Lots of money. Your face on the magazine covers. Everything."

I couldn't help but grin. That was the kind of thing Mom, Dad, and I talked about virtually every day. It filled our dinner conversations.

Pastor Rhodes gestured with his right hand, a tiny jab of challenge. "I think you should put *that* on the table and then make a decision."

My brow wrinkled. "That doesn't make any sense. All of that probably won't happen. It's a thousand-to-one long shot. Why should I make that my yardstick?"

My new friend's voice softened. "I'll tell you why, Ken. I think every day now about what Jesus Christ did for me. How He gave up more than Hollywood, more than fame, more than movie headlines. He sacrificed everything there possibly is in order to come down here and save Jo and me. And you see, that's a real story, man. I didn't make it up. Everything you heard in that tent is raw truth. *Real truth.*"

He went on, telling me in a quiet, careful voice how he envisioned heaven was going to be. Not just the mansions and the wide, pleasant streets paved with gold. Not just the sparkling, dancing ripples on the sea of glass. Not just the banquet tables laden with all of heaven's choicest menu selections. But the joy of worshiping Jesus, of bowing low before Him and thanking Him for Calvary. Of being with friends and loving family members for a safe eternity, where the scramble for position and a few glib words of insouciant praise were no longer needed. Where time itself was a friend and not an insistent enemy.

"Ken," he said, "I think if you put up this world's highest offers against Jesus' gift of heaven and grace and forgiveness—man, it is simply no contest. This world's greatest riches are not going to stand up against the goodness of Jesus. In my heart I know it; in your heart you know it too."

I realized something in a stunning and wonderful rush of emotion. After eight years of riding around in limousines and appearing before movie cameras with Alfalfa Switzer and Darla Hood next to me, I was now ready to make this eternal decision in a preacher's cramped little kitchen. There were no agents around to press me, no studio moguls to dangle their ephemeral promises. God had brought me to this crossroads on a cool Friday evening and had provided a friend to take me to the path of righteousness.

"What do you say, my friend?" The pastor took both of my hands and gave me a strong squeeze that sent heaven's power surging into my soul. I nodded. "I think I'm ready." Catching myself, I looked at both of them there in that kitchen and corrected my statement. "I know I'm ready."

Driving home I switched off the radio and simply listened to the voice of God whispering to me through the valley breezes. The highway took a sharp dip to the right as I crested the last hill before Hollywood, and the soft, elegant lights of my former world came into view.

On the right side of the freeway, a huge spotlight pierced the heavens, announcing yet another film premiere at Hollywood's legendary Grauman's Chinese Theater. At this very moment, low-slung limousines were delivering their jewel-laden cargo into the busy thoroughfare, where gushing crowds pressed forward and snapped worshipful pictures.

I smiled to myself, finally at peace, and turned the Chevy into our quiet boulevard.

Fade to black.

Chapter Fifteen

WALDO'S BEST ROLE

The overhead fan's slow rotation did little to stir the humid air in the church. I traced my bare big toe in the thin layer of dust on the wooden floor and then squinted up at the pulpit, where Dad was laboring through the conclusion of his sermon. His Thai vocabulary was still growing, and he sometimes paused to strain for a forgotten word. A diminutive native, Chalaw, who spoke some English, would occasionally murmur a prompt when he could tell what Dad, in beginner's Thai, was trying to say.

Danny, sitting next to me, was coloring a picture of Elijah getting food from the ravens, meticulously tracing in the blue sky and the dark wings on the birds as they dive-bombed the prophet with pieces of bread. "Is it almost over?" he stage-whispered to Mom, who adjusted the baby in her arms as she nodded Yes. She and Dad had spent the last eight months in an intensive language-study program, and she had just returned the other day from a successful foray to the open-air food market in Chiang Mai.

We all stood to sing the closing hymn, "In a Little While We're Going Home." Christians of various denominations throughout Thailand used the same hymnal, which contained several hundred

It's a long way from Hollywood— but there's nothing more elegant than my dad baptizing Thai young people in a mountain stream.

translated songs. Thai gospel singing made no attempt at rhyming the words, and I had to content myself with humming along. At the age of three, I wasn't yet ready to read—in either language.

Seconds after the closing prayer, there was a hubbub of noise from across the street. A paved two-lane road separated our little white church from several residential houses built in the Thai architectural style, and the one directly across from us had a large and overgrown yard. A bevy of Thai boys were pointing and shrieking, *"Ngu! Ngu!"*

"What is it?" I asked Mom.

"They found a snake," she told me. Cobras were common throughout northern Thailand, and we had to keep a close watch everywhere we went. The venomous reptiles would slither into front yards and even ease into kitchens if a door was left ajar.

"Can we go watch?" Danny was bursting with excitement.

"OK. But be real careful. Maybe see if Daddy can go with you."

I saw that Dad was still at the back door, greeting all of our members and visitors with the traditional *wai* greeting, a slight bow with both hands pressed together near one's chin. We slipped past him and darted across the street.

A tall kid wearing a tattered T-shirt proclaiming the thirst-quenching properties of Pepsi-Cola had a menacing stick, and he was creeping close to his prey. Five or six smaller children edged forward, hissing, *"Rawang! Antharai!"* ("Careful! It's dangerous!") After a few moments of wordless feinting, he suddenly gave a sharp, deadly whack with his stick, and a cheer went up. Dangling the lifeless corpse of the hooded snake on his stick, he did a victory dance. *"Chai-o!"*

"Is it dead?" I asked.

"Uh-huh." Danny was five and a lot bolder than I was. I squinted through my glasses at the colorful scene. Two of the little boys in the cheering section had just come from a morning of swimming and were completely naked in the noontime heat. Bathing *au naturel* was a common sight, and tots of both genders freely walked the streets of this primitive town after their morning swims. Several waved cheerfully to us as Dad clumsily shifted gears left-handed on our secondhand Jeep; it was a dusty ride back to our missionary home on Radjakpakinai Road.

In my dad's world of film, what you just experienced on this page would be called a "jump cut." In an abrupt and blurry moment, twelve years have passed, and you have a different author. Let me explain.

Waldo is my father. He grew up to have four sons; I'm the second of them. This book is his story. I thank God every day that I have the privilege of putting the words down on paper. But what I have shared with you is the gracious and relentless pursuit of the Holy Spirit, bringing my dad to his true calling in life.

Dad drove home from that Van Nuys meeting in 1946 with a determination to follow Jesus Christ and to serve Him. By the time I was born into this story, we were living in the very heart of a primitive mission field, ninety-five hundred miles away from Southern California. The Hollywood empire was fifteen time zones away; communication between the two worlds was impossible except by airmail letters, which took weeks to make the trip across the Pacific.

So clearly Dad's promise to God is one he kept. But here is the story.

He got home that Friday evening and found his parents still up, chatting over a late supper; Dennis was already in bed. Ken sat down with his folks and, without preamble, blurted out his decision, "I want to be baptized."

His mother was the first to speak. "Well, honey—my goodness. This is kind of sudden. Is this because of those meetings you've been going to? Over in Van Nuys?"

"Uh-huh."

She absorbed this. "Are you sure? You better tell us more about it first."

He nodded. "Yeah. I think what they teach is true and I like it. It's all from the Bible and makes a lot of sense. Plus, my friend Tony—well, he's an Adventist, and I just think he's a really good guy. It helps him."

His father, finishing up a helping of meatloaf, eyed the teenager. "Fine with me," he said at last. "You're old enough to make that decision. I don't mind."

Mom leaned over and gave Ken a pat on the hand. "Sweetheart, of course you know that I was raised in the Adventist Church. Somehow, it never took hold for me, but in my heart I have a lot of respect for people who want to make that a part of their lives. And your grandpa will be pleased, I know." She paused. "Do you want to wait a while, 'cause he'll probably be out here to visit, maybe next summer? He could baptize you then."

My dad thought about it for a moment, remembering how Grandpa had driven him to church and sent him all those letters through the years. "I don't know," he managed. "Yeah, that would be kind of good." He was about to say that the tent evangelist was already planning a baptism for the very next Sunday, but somehow he held back.

His father, deep in thought, suddenly leaned forward. "I gotta say," he managed, "that I kinda would like to have you hold up a bit. I mean, if it's what you want, fine. But this is some guy preaching in a tent."

"Yeah. So?"

His father slowly got up from his seat and stacked a pile of teetering dishes, carrying them to the sink. He returned and resumed his pitch. "Well, look," he said. "It's been a while, but when I was younger, living in Colorado, we went to this big cathedral church. They did good work, I recall. Food programs for the hungry and so on." He pointed out toward the distant lights of Burbank. "I noticed a few weeks ago that the same group has a nice church right over by Toluca Lake. You might think about joining them. It'd be a lot closer to home."

It took just a moment for my dad to sense the flaw in the invitation. "Pop," he said, graciously declining the delay, "if it was all that meaningful, you'd still be going there yourself. It's not much of a testimonial if you want me to join something you don't even care about."

His father's jaw tightened, but he said nothing.

Sunday evening my dad accepted a ride from Tony, and they rode out to Van Nuys together. Without saying anything to his parents, he had quietly packed a small athletic bag with a change of clothes and put it inside the back door to the garage. At the conclusion of Pastor McComas's sermon, he stepped into the pool with seven or eight other candidates and was baptized by immersion.

"I'm so proud of you, man," Tony said afterward, giving my dad a comradely punch on the arm.

"Thanks. I probably wouldn't have gotten to this point without you."

For at least two months, he kept his choice as a quiet secret between him and the Lord. He still attended church in Van Nuys each weekend, but his baptismal certificate was kept in the bottom of one of his drawers at home. Life at Hollywood High continued as he marched toward graduation.

One Friday evening after a family supper, the four of them were chatting when his mother quietly laid the simple sheet of paper in front of him. "Sweetheart, I found this in your room today," she explained, "while I was putting your laundry away." She put a hand on his shoulder. "I promise you I wasn't nosing around. Just, you know, all the clothes."

"Oh." Ken gulped. "Uh . . . is it all right?"

She nodded. "Well, of course, you know I thought it would have been nice for your grandpa to do your baptismal service. But I imagine you didn't want to wait."

"Huh-uh." He explained to both his parents how the pastor had already scheduled the baptism as a culminating celebration to the series of meetings and that he felt God calling him right at that moment. "I just wanted to do it while I was feeling God inviting me."

The moment of slight tension passed quickly as Dennis chimed in with some childish bit of silliness. Ken's mother came over and gave her older son a kiss on the top of his head. "You're a good kid," she murmured. "You can take Dennis with you to church if you want."

The issue of my dad's film career lay untouched for the time being. The indomitable Mr. Sherril, not sensing anything amiss, gave him a call a few months later. "Nothing big yet," he admitted, "but the office just let me know they got another two-day gig you might like."

Despite his resolve, Dad asked out of force of habit, "Like what?"

The older man checked his notes. "Back at MGM. Coupla lines, I hear. In some comedy. And I think they want someone who can play the piano a bit. You play, right?"

"Yeah." Dad tried to get up his courage to reject the part out of hand, but his newfound Christianity was still fragile. "Not great, but I can get by."

"That's great, kid! From what I hear, it's like fifteen seconds of some little thing, not much harder than 'Row, Row, Row Your Boat.' Shall I set you up?"

Dad paused, feeling a twinge of shame. "Yeah. Sure."

He drove himself to the studio the following afternoon, feeling turmoil as the security guard waved him through. "Long time no see, Waldo!"

"You too." He made his way over to the casting area where an assistant director explained the scene. "You stand here, you walk here, Miss Hamilton says blah, blah, blah, you say back, blah, blah, blah, and then you sit down at the piano and say right into the camera, 'And here's my response to *that!*'"

Dad nodded numbly. He glanced at the sheet music the assistant director had thrust into his hand. A few simple chords and a melody line any third-year piano student could play blindfolded.

"Shall we try it?" A stand-in actress stepped forward ready to prompt him through his single line of dialogue.

"Whenever you're ready, Kaye."

He pivoted on cue, grinned at the girl, said his line, and then eased over to the piano. Setting the music in place, he mugged for the camera. "And here's my response to *that!*" The stagehands chuckled; some of them, old-timers, remembered their own Waldo moments from years past.

Dad's hands poised over the keys. The notes on the page were simple: quarter notes and rests. The key of G—one sharp. *Mary had a little lamb* . . .

Dad and his younger brother, Dennis, enjoy time with their doting parents in Hollywood.

He couldn't do it. His hands were frozen over the keys.

"Whenever you're ready, Mr. Kaye. No cameras, no pressure."

Just press those keys down and get your two hundred and fifty dollars.

He couldn't do it. His hands would not play. His mind, diligently sending the signals to the noncompliant fingers, was somehow not transmitting. He tried to press down, but there was nothing.

"Come on, kid. Time's passing here. We don't want to give these people time and a half just 'cause of you. Let's hear some music."

Just this one last gig, Lord, and I'll walk away from this town forever. Let me play these notes, and then I'm Yours. Nothing. His fingers just wouldn't work.

Dad slowly stood up from the bench and shook his head. "I'm really sorry," he managed. "I guess it's just not my day."

"You sure, kid?" People in Hollywood were used to busted tryouts. "Want to try it again from the top?"

Dad shook his head. "No. Sorry. It's just—this one's not for me."

The assistant director took the sheet music out of his hand. "All right, bub. Sorry about that."

"Sure."

Dad drove back home filled with a kind of anxious joy. Was he done for good now?

That evening, after his little brother had been put to bed, he told his parents what had happened. "Oh, doll, that's too bad," his father said. "But it happens to the best of 'em. You'll get back on the horse and ride."

He shook his head. "You don't understand," he managed. "I'm done. I'm not going in any more."

"Hold on." His father sat up straight. "What are you talking about?"

"Just what I said." Dad took a deep breath and said an inward prayer. "It was great, I had a marvelous time, you guys supported me, and—I mean, I'm not sorry that was my life for a while. Waldo and the whole thing. But I'm not doing it any longer."

"How come?" Mom wanted to know, her voice gentle as if she suspected what was about to come.

Dad looked out of the kitchen window for a moment, toward the distant plains of Nebraska. Finally, he explained. "Grandpa has told me lots of times that God has something special for me to do. I don't know yet what it is, but I know for sure it's not making B movies."

"Oh, come on," his father scoffed. "Honey, you can be a Christian and still make movies. Lots of people do."

"Maybe so. But *I* can't."

His father's voice rose. "Kid, do you have any idea what this movie money has meant to the four of us?" He gestured around the beautifully decorated house. "Your little Waldo games bought this house, young man. Paid for this kitchen. Made sure we had food in the fridge

206 / Finding Waldo

all these years. And it was work for us too, sport. Your mama driving you down to MGM and waiting in the sun all day out by the lake while you and Darla rode around in toy boats. That's how we got where we are." He snorted. "Now you want to quit all that just 'cause somebody lights a cigarette in some movie?"

Dad took a breath. "Look, Pop," he said softly, "I love you guys. You know that. And I'm glad we all did well because of the lucky break of my being in movies. But it's over now. That's all. I'm trying to be a Christian, and that just doesn't go too well in Hollywood." He pulled his chair closer and described the scene in Wisconsin. "There were girls there, and I don't have to go into the details of all that was going on after hours. There was booze just everywhere you turned. Gambling. And the swearwords were something else." His voice shook a bit with emotion. "I got home from that thing, and after a while found out that all those words were in my head now too." He gestured with his head toward the garage. "I was out there just last week, trying to put away Dennis's bike and I bumped my shins on Mom's car. All of a sudden, *blank, blank, blank.* I didn't mean to, but all these dirty words rolled out right in front of Dennis. It about killed me."

His father sagged. "So what are you telling me?" he said dourly. "You can't just work on *good* movies?"

My dad shook his head with renewed determination. "Look," he confessed, "*Best Foot Forward* was a good movie. Clean, funny. Nothing bad about it. It's just that on the set, they're all danger. It doesn't matter what the film is; you've got technicians cussing and having sex while they're working on *Bambi.*"

His mother let out a little gasp at the raw outburst and my dad retreated. "I'm sorry, Mom," he managed. "But that's just how the industry is. It's a godless place. Nobody means for it to be so dark out there; it just is. And I'm like the baby-est Christian in the world. I can't make it that way."

The Smith family in Bangkok in 1967. Dad was chaplain of the Adventist hospital.

Her husband drummed his fingers in angry frustration on the table. "Well, just do some more thinking," he said at last. "Have you thought about the possibility that a whole lot more than Waldo money might someday come your way? That Jackie Coogan law is just waiting to make you rich."

Back in 1939, after *Our Gang*er Coogan and other child actors had ended up penniless because their parents frittered away all the earnings, legislators had debated certain safeguards designed to protect youngsters who toiled in the film industry. Now his dad pointed toward the calendar. "The way rules are heading, bud, any checks coming in now will be mostly yours to keep. The one perfect casting call comes along, and you're a millionaire. But not if you walk away."

My dad related his Friday night conversation with Pastor Rhodes. "If I trade in God and Jesus and heaven for the biggest role in the world, then I've blown it. Doesn't matter what movie part I have to give up—Jesus is bigger than any of them."

It was hard to argue with that sentiment, and the evening ended with an uneasy truce.

After graduation from Hollywood High School, his life took a risky turn when he signed up for a two-year stint in the army. Military life can be a challenge for the novice believer, even though the nation was in a rare moment of tranquility. Dad ended up being shipped over to Korea a few years before tensions there escalated into combat.

Tender as he was in his new beliefs, Dad felt prompted by the Lord to seek out a Christian home even in Seoul. A nearby church where sermons were preached in English embraced him warmly, inviting him regularly to services and colorful social events, and he returned to the United States nurtured in his commitment to God.

As his army hitch was completed, he faced yet another moment of decision. Mr. Sherril, always in regular contact on behalf of the acting agency, let him know there was still regular work to be had. But Dad, his resolve bolstered by the two years of independent hardness in soldiering, found it easier to move away from his former life. Once again, God's amazing grace manifested itself as he made his next choice.

A unique Adventist family, bursting with vitality and preaching power, had come upon the scene in the early 1900s. The Venden brothers, an evangelism duo, had crisscrossed America, holding tent meetings and stirring thousands to seek Christ. Dan and Melvin Venden were dynamic preachers who knew the gospel and who combined great Bible teachings with twinkle-in-the-eye social skills. Now a new generation of Venden talent was coming of age. Five cousins, all about the same age, were starting college together. Lou and Morris, both destined to follow in their father's footsteps, had enrolled in ministerial classes at La Sierra College, about an hour east of the Holly-

Dad and his bride, Jean Venden, embark on a most improbable life adventure together after saying Goodbye to Tinseltown.

wood studios. Dad, after weighing his options, signed up for the same school.

While there, he met his Jean, another of the Venden tribe. In between his own classes in theology and biblical languages, he fell in love and married into a family brimming with godly DNA and a passion for sharing Jesus with lost people.

As a new pastoral couple, the starry-eyed lovers interned at a couple of Adventist churches in Palm Springs and Escondido after graduating. They also made regular trips to the maternity ward. One weekend, while attending a spiritual rally in San Francisco, the guest evangelist asked the crowd: "Who in this audience is willing to say to the Lord right now, 'Jesus, if You want to send me, I'll serve You anywhere'?"

After looking at each other and reflecting on what the story of Calvary had meant to them, Mom and Dad both stood without hesitation. Not many months later, they found themselves on board the *Steel Admiral,* a merchant ship bound for what the missionaries were

Dad is ordained as a minister in the Seventh-day Adventist Church in 1956. A Pastor Baker presides.

still calling Siam. All my parents had heard about this exotic, faraway country was what most Americans knew from the popular musical, *Anna and the King of Siam,* starring Rex Harrison and Irene Dunne (ironically directed by the same John Cromwell Dad knew from his brief part in 1940's *Victory*). They had to literally look on a map to discover the distant world to which this diesel-belching ship was going to be taking them.

I was a two-year-old toddler, so I have no recollection of the cramped and rumbling cabins we shared during the six-week voyage. But my father, who used to wear tuxedos and tap-dance with stars like Darla Hood, who used to autograph eight-by-ten glossies for his fans, who used to get mentioned in *Variety* magazine, stood on the deck of a freighter one chilly evening and watched the lights of San Francisco slowly recede into the inky blackness of the lonely Pacific Ocean. Six weeks later, he and his bride stood, overwhelmed, in a faraway town where the road signs were foreign and where flies buzzed over the grimy outdoor market.

Chiang Mai was the world I grew up in. For years I didn't comprehend or appreciate that my dad, a former movie star, was now hacking paths through the jungle as he visited little villages and preached the gospel. He baptized new believers in rushing mountain streams. He visited orphanages and held branch Bible schools for runny-nosed, half-naked tots who gathered around to hear him explain in halting Thai about a loving God who had created them and who loved them.

My parents' home is filled with scrapbooks telling the saga of a life given to proclaiming Jesus Christ in a world of lostness. Scores of old black-and-white photos show men and women lined up to enter a watery grave and embrace the hope of Christianity. In a world where Buddhist philosophy and animist fears held sway, Waldo, the former actor, brought the good news of redemption and Calvary's offer of a home in heaven. The pile of baptism photos grew through the years of work.

After several years in Chiang Mai, we moved to Ubol, a small town near the border of Cambodia and not far from where a deadly conflict was developing with Vietnam. But the bulk of our service was eventually in Bangkok, where Dad served as a pastor and as the chaplain of the Adventist hospital. I attended a small mission school there, took violin lessons, went on camping trips, and learned how to water-ski in the Gulf of Thailand at what is now the infamous Pattaya Beach.

Sometimes on Friday afternoons, after school, Dad would take us to play golf in the sweltering heat. I still remember getting to play at a beach community called Hua Hin; the holes were torturously long, almost par sixes. Dan and I would flail away at our balls, often having to report a score of eleven or twelve on a single hole. At the end of hole five, though, there was a soda pop stand where you could buy ice-cold grape Fanta for two *baht,* the equivalent of ten cents.

The nuclear Smith family about the year 2000. Dad lived for these times with his four boys.

Occasionally, the hospital staff would rent Disney films from a local distributor, and we would all convene on the tennis court for our own version of Sunday night at the movies. One of the shorts that was available through the agency was entitled *The Kid From Borneo,* and all the missionary kids howled with laughter at the *Our Gang* classic. They didn't realize that their own Pastor Smith was best friends with the chubby kid named Spanky, who was running in terror from the savage on the screen growling, "Yum-yum! Eat 'em up!"

Dad stayed in mission work for a total of seventeen years, ending his career of Thailand service in 1974. We routinely saw newspaper clippings from the United States, sometimes emanating from Hollywood, marveling that a star from *Our Gang* was toiling for Christ in this remote corner of the world.

His return to America coincided with the college years of his sons. All four of Waldo's boys ended up in some form of pastoral service. My brothers all lead successful Adventist congregations, and I have spent the bulk of my career writing scripts for *Voice of Prophecy* and *It*

Is Written. Dad continued to minister at various churches throughout California, beaming with pride and officiating as we all married and presented him with nine grandchildren.

For years, Dad and I mused about the possibility of sitting down and writing a book together. At family gatherings we would enjoy watching *Three Men in a Tub*, but in all honesty, I never sensed what a rich and colorful story this really was. Dad spoke about it with affectionate recollections but never dwelled on his Hollywood past or on the myriad of juicy details that I'm sure were still in his memory bank. He never bragged about the successes he'd enjoyed and seemed genuinely thankful that the Lord had given him a far better life.

On Mother's Day 2002, most of us convened in Riverside to celebrate Mom's seventy-third birthday. We went to a nearby mall and had some Jamba Juice treats together and played games around the kitchen table. Dad was still an inveterate entertainer, and he kept his grandsons in stitches with his relentless comedy and self-deprecating humor about the cards he was being dealt. I backed out of their driveway that evening, seeing their retreating forms in my rearview mirror. What a rich life the Lord had given to Waldo!

Three days later, I was working on radio scripts when I got a frantic phone call. Dad had been struck from behind by a hit-and-run driver. He was hovering between life and death in the Intensive Care Unit of Riverside Community Hospital. Our hearts in our throats, Dan and I motored our way across Los Angeles to where our mother was waiting. All four of Dad's sons were at his bedside as the sterile machines hummed and the doctors labored in a futile attempt to hold back the forces of death. We read God's promises of resurrection found in 1 Thessalonians 4, the sure words of hope about a new life in God's eternal kingdom. We held hands and prayed in thanksgiving that Dad had chosen a life away from the facade of fame and glitter that promised so extravagantly but could not deliver.

Mom, my three brothers, all Adventist pastors, and I are at Dad's funeral in May of 2002.

Waldo passed away at eight forty that evening. I drove my mother home, numb with grief, and called my wife and daughters to tell them what had happened. Early the next morning, I realized that considering his *Our Gang* history, this was a story with national importance. Scribbling down some thoughts, I made a few phone calls, and soon the AP wire services were informing the world that a child prodigy named Waldo, who had brought pleasure to so many, had been struck down at the age of seventy-two.

At the funeral ten days later, La Sierra University Church was packed as we said Goodbye to our dad. His life in *Our Gang* was celebrated; some bits of humor about Waldo were enjoyed. But the enduring message from this actor's four sons was of the hope that comes through Jesus Christ. A choir sang the "Hallelujah" chorus and a wonderful men's chorale, Christian Edition, performed one of my favorites, "Soon and Very Soon."

Many times while he was living, people asked my dad this obvious question: "Pastor Smith, do you regret your choice? You could have hung around Hollywood and still had that big moment happen." Borrowing from an old Brando line, "You coulda been *somebody!*" Had Waldo made the right choice?

Now that Dad is gone, the question sometimes falls to me. What do I think?

Ironically, I respond by choosing instead to tell the rest of Alfalfa's story.

This freckle-faced kid was clearly Dad's superior in acting talent. He got the big parts and he was known around the world. He could twist his face into an amazing array of emotions, and be funny just by standing there. Darla later told friends: " 'Once, when he left [the studio] at the end of the day, I remember Clark Gable and Alfalfa went out through the gate at the same time, and people made a bigger fuss over Alfalfa. I saw it happen.' "[1] After leaving *Our Gang,* it was an obvious decision to loiter around Hollywood and try to cash in on the cachet of being Alfalfa.

And yet film success, always a fickle lover on Sunset Boulevard, somehow eluded my father's prickly friend. With the Frank Capra connection that both of them enjoyed, he managed to get a smallish part in one of the world's most popular films, *It's a Wonderful Life.* Later, Dad was already slogging through rice paddies in Thailand when Carl Switzer was able to get some film work in the acclaimed prison drama *The Defiant Ones,* with Sidney Poitier and Tony Curtis, getting the bit part of a character named Angus.

Beyond that, it seemed that he simply could not escape the shackles of being a tone-deaf crooner. Everything he did was temporary and noneventful. He drifted into a frustrating existence of tending bar, and occasionally taking tourists on guided hunting expeditions in northern California. Everywhere he went, people would holler, "Hey, Alfalfa!" Rude fans would ask him to sing off-key for them. His *Our Gang* work brought no royalties and, soon, no job offers. He bumped around trying to find work; there were rumors that he had gotten busted for growing pot. He got married, but the relationship soon fell apart.

We were still living in Thailand when a faded news clipping arrived from my grandparents. Incredibly, several years after the bitter disappointment of their Waldo leaving the lucrative world of film, Dad's own parents had experienced their own epiphany and accepted Jesus Christ as well. What a great blessing to attend the local Adventist church with them each time we were on a brief furlough to America. Now my grandpa sent Dad a story about the demise of his childhood friend.

As the tragic saga goes, Switzer had borrowed a hunting dog from a friend, "Bud" Stiltz. The dog had gotten lost, but eventually showed up, and somehow Alfalfa had had to pay fifty dollars to the person who returned it. He got it in his mind that Stiltz should reimburse him for the financial loss. He arrived at the man's house in a hot temper, flashed a fake police badge, and somehow gained entrance. When he demanded the refund, a violent argument ensued. Alfalfa bashed the other man over the eye; soon his adversary retreated to a bedroom and emerged with a gun. There was a sweaty grappling for the weapon, and shots were fired that missed both parties. Somehow, Alfalfa pulled a knife, tried to stab the other man, and it was then that Stiltz managed to get off a shot, fatally wounding the thirty-one-year-old actor. He died of blood loss while being driven to the hospital. The shooting was ruled to be justifiable homicide, and Dad's long-time movie pal was laid to rest in the year 1959—in Hollywood's Forever Cemetery.

I know that other movie careers end with more glory than Alfalfa's. You can go online and read *Our Gang* stories: some of them long, others tragically short. Some made many more films and lived in the lap of luxury; others died penniless.

What about Dad? For seventeen years, while Alfalfa was chasing his elusive dreams, my father was baptizing Thai teenagers. He was giving Bible studies to migrant workers and young women rescued from the brothels of Bangkok. He was taking the youth from our Chiang Mai church on spiritual retreats, camping trips to the beach, teaching them to sing "Amazing Grace" around the campfire.

Forty years later, I have taken trips back to my homeland. Bangkok has a brand-new airport, Suvarnabhumi Airport, which is elegant and state of the art. Digital screens are everywhere, and you can plug in your laptop and get wireless signals. I retreat from the muggy heat to an air-conditioned hotel room where I can watch *Law and Order* and get the Fox News Channel before going to bed.

But then Mom and I will travel to a church for a reunion. There are gray-haired men and women, slower in their gait now, who were baptized by Waldo when they were teenagers. They introduce us to their children and grandchildren, all faithful in the still embryonic Christian church that is slowly growing in the land of Buddhist smiles. They tell us how God has blessed them, how their understanding of grace and Calvary has made their lives complete. And they hold up their hands in that beautiful, gracious Thai gesture, the *wai*, which is a wonderful expression of love and respect—and perhaps even gratitude.

This is why I felt the Lord calling me to tell this story. If it were just to summarize an eight-year bit career in the movies, I would not have bothered. Dad never wrote down his memories, and he didn't dictate his minor glories into a tape recorder—probably because he didn't think it was worth the bother either. Frankly, if you want to feed on MGM trivia, you could simply surf the net or read Leonard Maltin's wonderful book and get a clear picture of the sets, the sight gags, the romantic plays, and the interplay between Alfalfa, Butch, and Waldo. Someone with a stopwatch could easily clock how much total Hal Roach *Our Gang* time Waldo had on-screen compared to

Alfalfa's three hours and fifty-eight minutes; but who cares? It was a cute career and the final credits roll; please deposit your trash in the container on your way out of the theater.

But it really took the tragic loss in 2002 before I finally comprehended what God had done here. At Dad's funeral there were four sons, all wanting to share poignant memories, so I only had about five minutes to choke back my tears and say something from the heart. I spoke about this choice and also about the amazing richness of Dad's life. His years were filled with color, with adventure, with lasting love, with travel and beauty and a mosaic of world influence and trusted friends. Not to mention fifty-one years of love and companionship with a beautiful and godly wife whose heart throbbed in unison for their shared spiritual adventures. "Dad's entire life was golden," I observed, "because his friendship with God was golden." And this is something I wish I had noticed much earlier.

After he passed away, part of Dad's library came into my possession. He had underlined great portions of C. S. Lewis's books, and one paragraph from *The Weight of Glory* exposes the great paradox of our shortsighted values. "If we consider the unblushing promises of reward and the staggering nature of the rewards promised in the Gospels, it would seem that Our Lord finds our desires not too strong, but too weak. We are half-hearted creatures," he writes, "fooling around with drink and sex and ambition when infinite joy is offered us, like an ignorant child who wants to go on making mud pies in a slum because he cannot imagine what is meant by the offer of a holiday at the sea. We are far too easily pleased."[2] It is easy—too easy—to comfortably drift into the first pleasant life that offers itself to us especially if it comes with a dose of adulation or a movie producer's envelope filled with dollar bills.

I was charmed by a parallel anecdote from the *Our Gang* archives, again thanks to the painstaking reference work of Leonard Maltin. In

God blessed Dad with the opportunity to serve Him as a pastor and as a missionary in Thailand.

a delightful story that preceded Dad by five years, entitled *Readin' and Writin'*, a kid nicknamed Breezy Brisbane is loath to go back to school. Mom, of course, gives him the old bromide that if he studies hard and applies himself, he can be president someday. "I don't wanna be president," he grumps. "I wanna be a streetcar conductor." It's a baffling life goal until he explains cheerfully, "Boy, do *they* pick up the nickels!" And thereby, a destiny is made.

So I close this story by thinking about the what-ifs and then the choice Dad made. Today more than ever, Hollywood tells stories that enjoy one intensive *flash* of influence and then they quickly fade from view. Nickels on the floor of the streetcar, as it were. Anxious studio executives know that a huge first weekend on two thousand screens is their starry dream because after just a few weeks, even the blockbusters are dropped and new widescreen stories take their place. A scriptwriter gives his life to telling a story, and in three weeks, the film goes on a shelf somewhere at MGM. People jaded by their plasma flat screens are renting and purchasing fewer DVDs than ever, opting instead to surf the millions of channels that compete for their attention. I enjoy a good movie as much as anyone, but really, what *small* and easily erasable stories they usually seem to be.

Somehow, Dad, as a wistful teenager, heard the Lord's call through his grandpa's letters. With a wisdom beyond his years, he understood that he could participate in telling these small and temporary tales of lust and betrayal that flickered so briefly on movie screens. Or he could give his life to telling the one story that would survive for eternity in the redeemed lives of people around the world who loved Waldo as their pastor and their friend.

And so it was that Dad found his greatest role in life. By the way, I understand from reading his favorite script that Waldo will definitely be returning for the sequel.

Notes

Chapter 2: Screen Test
1. Rebecca Gulick, *Those Little Rascals: The Pictorial History of Our Gang* (New York: Crescent Books, 1993), 35.

Chapter 3: Soap Bubbles and Boxing Gloves
1. Leonard Maltin and Richard W. Bann, *The Little Rascals: The Life and Times of Our Gang* (New York: Crown Publishers, 1992), 101.

Chapter 4: Cue Cards and Crashes
1. Maltin and Bann, *The Little Rascals*, 51.

Chapter 5: Busted
1. Maltin and Bann, *The Little Rascals*, 128.
2. Ibid.
3. Ibid., 204; emphasis in the original.
4. Ibid., 271.

Chapter 6: Cinema Tricks
1. Maltin and Bann, *The Little Rascals*, 99.
2. Jackie Lynn Taylor, *The Turned-On Hollywood 7: Jackie Remembers Our Gang* (Toluca Lake, Calif.: Pacifica House, 1970), 31.

Chapter 8: Moving to Metro-Goldwyn-Mayer

1. Tommy "Butch" Bond and Ron Genini, *Darn Right It's Butch* (Wayne, Pa.: Morgin Press, 1994), 67, 68.
2. Maltin and Bann, *The Little Rascals*, 5.
3. Ibid., 7.
4. Ibid., 128; emphasis in the original.
5. Ibid., 164.
6. Ibid; emphasis in the original.

Chapter 9: Black and White in the Movies

1. Maltin and Bann, *The Little Rascals*, 107.
2. Gulick, *Those Little Rascals*, 21.
3. Maltin and Bann, *The Little Rascals*, 97.

Chapter 10: Hollywood's Fast Lane

1. Maltin and Bann, *The Little Rascals*, 156.
2. Ibid., 202.
3. Ibid., 196.
4. Ibid., 114.
5. Ibid., 203.

Chapter 11: Double Takes

1. Maltin and Bann, *The Little Rascals*, 271.
2. Ibid., 172.
3. Ibid.
4. Gulick, *Those Little Rascals*, 62.

Chapter 14: Final Credits

1. C. S. Lewis, *Surprised by Joy* (New York: Harcourt Brace Jovanovich, 1955), 216.

Chapter 15: Waldo's Best Role

1. Maltin and Bann, *The Little Rascals*, 270.
2. C. S. Lewis, *The Weight of Glory* (San Francisco, Calif.: HarperCollins Publishers, 1949), 26.

Additional Background References

Books
Richard Lamparski, *Whatever Became of . . . ?* 10th Series (New York: Crown Publishers, 1986).

Jackie Lynn Taylor, *The Turned-On Hollywood 7: Jackie Remembers Our Gang* (Toluca Lake, Calif.: Pacifica House, 1970).

Web sites
IMDB.com—Internet Movie Database

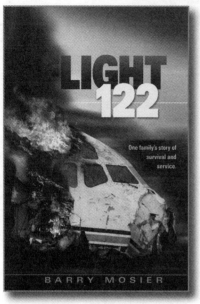
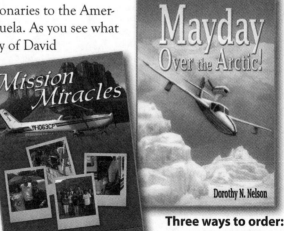